To / Jack

Rockfist gets his wings

How I made the grade
as a jet fighter pilot

by

Ralph C. Rutherford
with Hugh Frostick

with my very best wishes

Ralph C. Rutherford *Dec. 2018.*

First published in the United Kingdom in 2018 by
Frostick Publishing
17 Meadow Close, Great Bromley, Colchester CO7 7UG
www.frostick.co.uk
ISBN: 978-0-995-7938-4-2

Typeset by Frostick Publishing, Great Bromley
Printed and bound by CZ Design & Print,
Bishops Stortford 01279 657769

Contents

Foreword by Andy Cubin

Ralph Rutherford was my Geography teacher at high school during the late 1970s. He had a caring side that set him apart from most of his peers and I enjoyed his lessons because I liked him.

Having discovered that Ralph "Rockfist" Rutherford had been a fighter pilot in the RAF and with me becoming interested in aviation around that time, our conversations inevitably drifted to flying and Ralph's memories of his adventures in Meteors and Vampires. These conversations I would have gladly listened to for hours but I don't believe he took my own ambitions too seriously.

In 1994 I ran into Rockfist at North Weald Air Show where I was the RAF Jaguar display pilot. It was a thrilling reunion not least on my part, since I was quietly indebted to this man who enthused me to follow a career path which turned out to be so very successful. It was also the same weekend I met the woman I later married.

About ten years later I flew a group of veterans from Kemble to Elvington in support of Operation Propeller which is a gathering of flying veterans on an old airfield to celebrate... them! With a couple of hours to kill I was wandering about minding my own business when Rockfist appeared on the path in front of me. "Rockfist Rutherford, stand to attention!" came out of my mouth. That stopped him in his tracks and raised his eyebrows!

The intervening decade disappeared as Ralph invited me for tea and cake at the hospitality area, which he kindly let me pay for. By then I was an airline Captain which meant tea and cake had become a daily ritual, something else we seemed to have in common.

I've not seen him since then, but we stay in touch via email. He still likes to reminisce about his fighter days and I still wish his tales would last longer than a few words on the internet. Perhaps, with this book, it is time.

Sqn Ldr Andy Cubin MBE RAF Ret'd
RAF Jaguar Display Pilot 1994-1996
RAF Red Arrows 1997-1999

Dedication

I dedicate this book to Mollie, my dear wife for 67 years who put up with all my foibles in a most supportive way. I miss her so terribly.

Acknowledgements

"Heh way man, ah wi gannin oot the morrow neet? Git yor clogs on, should be a laff! A dinna wanna miss one laff. Dazz yor lass iver moan aboot us gannin out?"

The reader will probably glad to hear I decided not to write Geordie speak in my book, although I used and abused it for my first quarter century. Instead I have reverted to the King's English as best I can!

I thank all the folk who have shaped my life and helped me have such wonderful experiences, from family, school teachers and school friends, workmates, RAF colleagues and Air Crew chums, teaching colleagues and rewarding pupils, as well as all those folk sharing in my hobbies and interests of my retirement years.

I greatly appreciate all the staff of Marjorie Girling House for making Mollie's last few months with me so friendly, welcoming and comfortable.

I do have a propensity to forget names and some other facts may have got a bit muddled in my old age. I did want to record what I have read or heard of what my old chums (and otherwise) have been up to. Some of this is hearsay which means I can't be sure of it all. If anyone knows different or can offer further information about anything I have written, particularly the whereabouts of old friends, then I would be delighted to hear it and can be contacted through my publisher.

I do not have records of who gave me the photos that I did not take myself, and it has not been possible to check or ask permission for copyright which I hope I have not unwittingly infringed.

I thank Hugh for all his work in producing this book for me, Dorothy for her fine maps and Jemma for her marvellous cover painting.

I do hope you enjoy reading my story.

Ralph Crawford Rutherford
Felixstowe, April 2018

Glossary of terms, slang & abbreviations

2nd Dickie	New pilot observing an experienced pilot
2TAF	2nd Tactical Air Force
A/G	Air Gunner (Air crew who manned a gun)
ACRC	Air Crew Reception Centre
Air Cdre	Air Commodore
A-Level	Advanced Level school exam, usually taken aged 18. See O-level
AOC	Air Officer Commanding
ASF	Advanced Servicing Flight
ATC	Air Training Corps (Cadets)
AWOL	Absent without leave (skiving)
BAFO	British Air Forces of Occupation
BAOR	British Army of the Rhine
Bob	As in "a few bob" - a shilling
Brass / Top Brass	High ranking officers making the big calls
Chiefy	Chief Engineer (Ground crew)
Clippy	Conductor/ticket collector who clipped tickets
CO	Commanding Officer
CPO	Chief Petty Officer (RN)
Dene	Small wooded valley (Northumberland)
DFM	Distinguished Flying Medal
F/O	Flying Officer - a rank, but not necessarily a pilot
FIDO	Fog Investigation and Dispersal Operation - fuel burning system to lift fog and light a runway path
Flak	Anti-aircraft fire
Flt Lt	Flight Lieutenant
FRG	Federal Republic of Germany or West Germany
GCA	Ground Control Approach
GCI	Ground Controlled Interception
Geordie	Nickname for a person with Tyneside accent
George	Lancaster Auto-pilot
Ground crew	The chaps who prepared and repaired the planes
Groupie	Group Captain
Ha'penny	Half an old penny (½d)
IF	Instrument Flying
Jankers	punishment for violating service discipline
Kite	Pet name for aeroplane
LAC	Leading Aircraftman
LNER	London and North East Railway
MATS	Military Air Transport Service (US)
MID	Mentioned in Dispatches
MD	Managing Director

MO	Medical Orderly (Doctor)
MOD	Ministry of Defence
MT	Military Transport
MU	Maintenance Unit
MUG	Mid-upper gunner
NAAFI	Navy, Army and Air Force Institute, who provided supplies and catering for HM Forces
NCO	Non-commissioned officer, someone who has been promoted through the ranks
OFCA	Old Felixstowe Community Association
O-Level	Ordinary level school exams, usually taken aged 16. See A-level
Op	Operation or sortie, a mission to bomb the enemy
OTU	Operational Conversion Unit (learning to fly in combat situations)
P/O	Pilot Officer
PACT	Pre Air Crew Training
Penn'orth	A penny's worth (1d)
Peri track	Perimeter track, road encompassing an airfield
PII	Sergeant Pilot equivalent rank
POW	Prisoner of war
PT / PE	Physical Training / Education
R/T	Radiotelephony (wireless intercom from aircraft)
RAF	Royal Air Force
RDX	Research Department Explosive - a replacement for TNT originating from Woolwich Arsenal
RN	Royal Navy
Skipper	Man in charge (pilot of plane or captain of ship)
Sqn Ldr	Squadron Leader
Square bashing	Parade Drill
Tabs	Geordie slang for cigarettes
TB	Tuberculosis
Tuppence	Two pennies
USAAF	United States Army Air Force
VC	Victoria Cross
VE (day)	Victory in Europe, when the Nazis surrendered to the Allies.
VJ (day)	Victory over Japan, when the Japanese surrendered marking the end of the war
W/O	Warrant Officer, a senior NCO
WAAF	Women's Auxiliary Air Force, and Waafs were the ladies therein
Wad	A type of cake sold in the NAAFI
Wingco	Wing Commander
WW1	World War One

Chapter 1
Flash, bang... wallop?

I t is 1950 and the Cold War with Soviet Russia is on: tense times for a fresh young fighter pilot with the British Air Forces of Occupation in West Germany.

I was in my Mark V de Havilland Vampire, V for Victor, doing rocket practice. We had flown from RAF Gütersloh to our rocketing range at Nordhorn with eight rockets loaded. MOD funds were rather tight which meant we didn't get too many chances to fire the real thing.

Our Vampires on 16 Squadron were some of the oldest still flying. V-Victor had been playing up with a strange vibration and I was not happy with it. I had spoken to my ground crew who had carefully checked over the engine, yet they could find nothing wrong. It certainly ran up smoothly and seemed fine down on the ground but I had told them it was still not right. I knew they were starting to wonder if I was suffering from nerves and simply imagining problems that weren't there.

The Vampire was very quiet up the front. There was very little noise in the cockpit as all the roar was left far behind. The nose was very streamlined which meant there was just a gentle rushing of air and the pilot could easily hear things going on and the R/T intercom. V-Victor was just vibrating slightly for me, as usual.

The rockets were fired from a handle grip which was shaped like a sausage, with a red button on the end of it to press with your thumb. I was firing my rockets in pairs. I made my approach to line up my first shot on the ground target and the rockets went down very nicely. Not a direct hit, but close. I came round for my second go, got lined up and "hit the tit". There were bright flashes of sparks, an almighty bang, and a big cloud of smoke started filling the cockpit. I thought "Bloody hell, I'm on fire!"

On the R/T I called, "Liner One-Nine Mayday Mayday!" for a quick return to base. I slipped the hood open slightly to try to suck out the smoke and see if I could regain visibility.

I was wondering if this time, Rockfist had had his chips?

Chapter 2
Northumberland farmers

I was born in August 1926 and named Ralph Crawford Rutherford. My middle name came from one of father's neighbouring farming friends, Major Crawford, as my father was probably running short of names after all the children he'd had. I am the last of the eleven still alive.

My father Francis Rutherford was a farmer, as was his brother William. Between them and their children they owned a number of farms in and around Longhorsley, about twenty miles north of Newcastle-upon-Tyne in the Morpeth district of Northumberland. The main homestead where Francis lived was Fieldhead, and other family farms included Viewlaw, High Trewitly, Beacon Hill and Whinneyhill. Several of my older half-siblings were partners with him in the faming business.

His first marriage to Georgina produced Elizabeth, Frank, Tom, Will and Georgina. The second marriage to Mary produced John, Charles and Dorothy. My mother, Ethel Alice Smailes (or Smiles), then had three children with Francis, being Ethel Margaret known as Peggy, myself, and Andrew Septimus known as Sep who was the seventh son of Francis, hence his name. (A brief family tree is included in Appendix 1 but, fear not, this is not a family history!).

My mother came from Seghill some miles away. She had been in service in Newcastle where she lived in with all living expenses included which meant she only got paid 1s (one shilling) a week. She told me how it took her a long time to save up enough to buy a bicycle.

Morpeth was a very pretty market town on the River Wansbeck. There was a market day on Wednesdays (and probably other days) and every month or so they had a hirings day. Farmers came into town and workers also came in who were looking for a job. Anyone want a maid, a labourer, a stockman? I believe it was on one of these days that mother was employed by father as housekeeper after his second wife died. Ethel was a sturdy lass who would be strong enough to look after a big family and work hard feeding the pigs, calves and so on. She must have passed the test and so he married her.

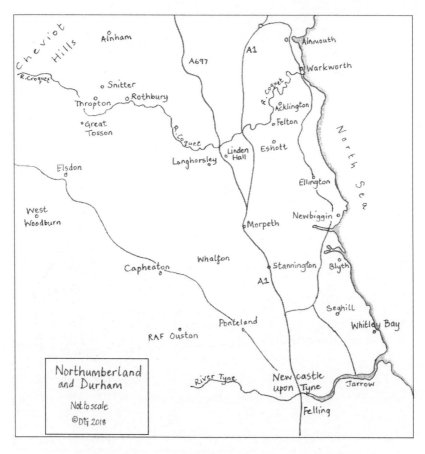

Map showing our part of Northumberland around Longhorsley,
the village where I was born, in the Morpeth District.
Also showing various of the family farms around
the River Coquet and other places I lived and visited
around Tyneside and Warkworth.

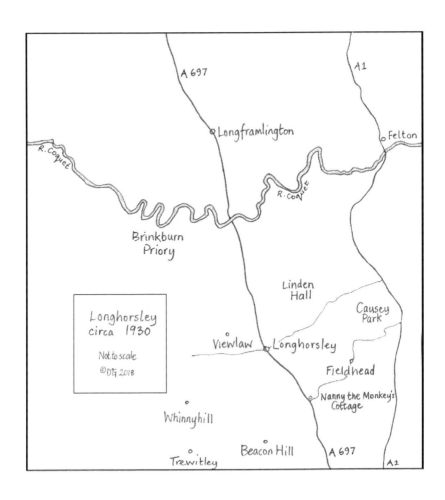

Larger map of Fieldhead farm in the Longhorsley area.
Uncle William farmed at Beacon Hill.
Viewlaw, Trewitley and Whinnyhill were other family farms.

Father (Da) and Mother (Mam) with my sister Peggy and one of the dogs at the front door of Fieldhead Farmhouse, at about the time I was born.

With the three marriages there were eleven of us children arising from Fieldhead and, the way things turned out, I didn't know some of my half-siblings very well at all. The first of them were thirty years older than me!

Father's eldest daughter, Elizabeth, was rather eccentric and was known to the younger ones as Nanna. I met her only the once on the way out of Miss Neil's ice cream shop. I was with my sister Dorothy who said to me, "This is Nanna." I said, "Hello" but Nanna didn't trouble to stop to reply to me.

She lived in Felton, near to Dorothy, on the other side of the River Coquet. One day when she was in her late seventies she reversed her car and somehow it slid down towards the river where the rear end got stuck in the water. She clambered out and went to find Mr. Jermy, a local haulier, who pulled it out of the river with his tractor. She thanked him and said, "I am going shopping in Alnwick," and off she went as if nothing had happened.

When Nanna's husband died, I am told that after the funeral she came back to the house with the mourners. She indicated, "There are

6

sandwiches and tea in there, do help yourselves." Then she went off to fetch a step ladder, pot of paint and a brush and she started painting the window frames.

My oldest brother Frank was another I only seldom met. Like Nanna he lived on the other side of the Coquet Valley on the outskirts of Thropton a few miles from Rothbury. One year I was holidaying with brother Charles who wondered if I would like to visit Frank on the other side of the River Coquet. There were some fords that could be used if the river was low but, on this occasion, we had to go all the way round to the bridge in Rothbury to get across the river.

Charles drove us up a very steep and rough old track to Frank's farm. Frank was married to a woman who seemed a bit of a simpleton, and he was not all that worldly himself, I thought, but that didn't stop him from making a lot of money.

As we entered the kitchen we could see on the other side a stable-type door with the top half open. A ruminating cow was standing there with its head in the kitchen. A chicken was standing on the table whilst others were running around below. The place was chaos!

Frank had two children, Rosemary and John. John became a policeman but contracted TB and died fairly young. Rosemary received a large inheritance when Frank died. She had married a chap my brother Charles didn't approve of and when Rosemary died her husband inherited the farm and money. My brother was very cross about this as he considered the husband to have "never done a day's work in his life." Not my concern, as I never saw any of them after that visit.

Tom I knew and liked well, and I will mention him later, and I am also fond of his son George.

I can remember nothing much about William and Georgina.

Of the children from the second marriage, John comes into my story, as do Charles and Dorothy. Charles farmed at Snitter (old English for snow) and in recent years he helped manage the farm belonging to the TV personality Robson Green who was involved in a good series about our home county of Northumberland. Charles married Hilda and poor Charlie found her dead in the toilet and had to get a ladder to climb in the window. I am in contact with their

7

daughter Audrey and her husband Tom Snaith at High Tosson. Sister Dorothy married Archie and I saw quite a lot of them.

My father Francis always wore a bowler hat and they say he owned the first private motorcar in Northumberland and that he once turned it upside down in a ditch!

Dad in his car, with men of the district. This photo was connected with "riding of the bounds" in about 1924. In those days they would ride round on horseback to find the marking stones to protect the parish boundaries

Father was on his third marriage and over sixty when I arrived at Fieldhead, and then I was only three and a half years old when he died in the operating theatre at 1, Park Road, Newcastle during a gallstone operation. That was a fairly routine procedure but I suppose all surgery in 1930 was a bit dodgy and clearly something went wrong. Peggy was only eight at the time and little Sep was not yet two.

I didn't know him long at all, but I still retain a few memories. Father kept collies and whippets like all farmers. I remember walking down to the duck pond and going around the cow byres with him and his dogs. I can picture him sitting on the step of the long byre, the milking shed that held twenty cows, sharpening a reaper blade. I remember the butcher, Jimmy McGregor from Choppington, who came to buy stock from our farm and would sometimes stay the afternoon with Dad to smoke pipes and play dominoes. I can still sing the hymn that my mother played on a record on the day of his funeral, *Will the angels play their harps for me.*

Dad and Peggy at the back door of the farm about 1926. The big slabs in the foreground covered a stream and a water pump

There was a crack between the sandstone slabs covering the pump in the stream. When I was about three I went to my mother's room and took her amber necklace, which was a beautiful thing with barrel shaped beads, large at the front and small at the back. Worth quite a lot of money I should think.

I don't know why I did it, but I dropped it down that crack in the stones! I suppose she must have missed it, but I was never questioned and certainly never volunteered any information about its disappearance.

Another funny thing that I don't remember doing myself, but my mother told me I had done, was when I was not much older. My parents bought me a schoolboy-style cap and when we arrived home I flung it straight in the fire. I have no idea why, but presumably I didn't want a hat!

Da looks very old in the pictures. But you did, back then, when you were in your sixties. I probably don't look as old as him even now, and I'm in my nineties!

Sadly, my mother was no longer so welcome in the house after father's death, being only a stepmother to most and a relative newcomer. She had been happily keeping house and cooking meals three times a day for ten or more hungry people, yet it seems they could not get rid of her quick enough. After Mam left the family home with us bairns (children), brother John kept Fieldhead and the other siblings gradually went their own way and bought other farms. My relatives still farm in the area.

John in about 1930

Father was a wealthy man who left £18,000 in his will. I didn't know it for some years, but Sep and I both had a legacy waiting for us when we reached the age of 21. I found out much later that Tom was an executor for Father's will and he was giving Mam the interest on our inheritance to keep us going. She needed the money and when I found out about the arrangement, I certainly didn't begrudge her having used "our" money to keep us clothed and fed.

10

I didn't know much about Longhorsley as we didn't go there a lot. Taking the little road west from our farm to the main road there was a cottage known as "Nanny the Monkey's cottage" on the junction. Why it was called that, nobody could tell me. We more often went the other way out from the farm towards Morpeth. Whilst our parents went shopping in the market town they left us with a Mrs Wetherell, a paid babysitter I suppose, who made the most delicious custard for Sep and me.

The local pub in Longhorsley was the Shoulder of Mutton. They had lots of little pictures around the walls and my father featured in many of them, as he had been quite a figure in the local farming community. When I revisited some years later they had all been taken down and so I asked the landlord what had happened to them. He told me they all went in the rubbish! I have never been able to understand the mindset of people who don't see the value in history. They would rather destroy something than bother to pass it on.

Outside the pub I encountered an old fellow who said, "Aareet lad. You're a stranger. Who are you?"

"I am Ralph Rutherford."

"Rutherford, eh? Do you belong to Fieldhead?"

I said that I did.

"Are you related to Francis Rutherford?"

"He was my father."

"Really! I used to play dominoes with your father. And do you know what? He would drink half a bottle of whisky as we played. When it came 10 o'clock, he wouldn't know where he was. We used to put him on his horse and send it home, three miles across the fields. He could not walk three yards but he could remain mounted on the horse."

Brother Charlie giving a visiting Boy Scout a ride on a cart horse

11

Chapter 3
Geordie Boy on Tyneside

When Mam was pushed off to Newcastle she ran a café in Northumberland Street, which is the main shopping road in the city centre forming part of the original A1 road. This was during the Great Depression but she seemed to make a living from it. In fact, Newcastle seemed to me to be a prosperous city. It was noisy and busy, although I was not aware of pollution from all the factories and shipyards and can remember no smogs.

Mother had a waitress called Daisy. I saw her one day skipping with a big string of sausages and my mother was sitting nearby and laughing her head off. Because Mam was a widow there was often a fellow hanging about who I expect was trying to court her.

The Café was upstairs, above a shop, and we lived in the third floor above that. One New Year's Eve I recall standing at the bedroom window watching the Highland Regiment pipe band come marching down Northumberland Street. It was wonderful, giving me my first insight into military music. The sounds took a long time to reach us and a long time to die away again; it was quite gorgeous.

Peggy and me

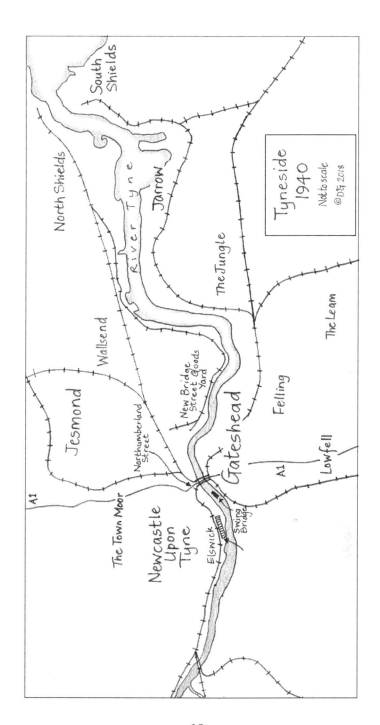

Dolcis Shoe Shop was opposite the café (or at least that was its location when I worked there ten years later). Next to that was Maynards sweet shop where I liked to go across for sweets. Maynards was a big company with lots of shops around the country. Their speciality was wine gums and they also had a toffee factory in Newcastle. One day when I walked over to the shop with my sixpence I saw four men outside. They were very ragged, poor devils; one had lost an arm and two had lost legs, presumably being wounds from the Great War. They were holding out a tin to beg for money but I didn't help them as I needed my sixpence for sweets.

For some reason mother gave up the café and moved to Felling-on-Tyne, south of the river, where she became the steward of the British Legion Club. There she met John Finlay, a miner who was out of work, and she married him – a bloody big mistake in my view, but there we are. We called our stepfather Pop Finlay. Mother and Pop together had three children called Ella, Robert and John.

Pop Finlay, as cheerful as ever, with Sep and Ella

My half-brother Robert died of meningitis at only one year old, in great pain. Mam said she could hear him crying even when she was arriving outside the Fleming Memorial Hospital in Jesmond. Because it cost a bit to visit Robert every day, she got me to go to a local newsagent who rang the hospital to ask how he was and I brought the answer back to her on a piece of paper. One morning when I handed her the note she burst out crying. Robert was dead. Very sad days, they were.

Our first home in Felling was a lovely semi-detached house at Number 12, The Avenue. I suppose the rent was too much as we then moved to a flat in a very old and run-down area, Number 16 Church Street on the corner opposite the Catholic church.

Felling was a much poorer area and rather grubbier than the city centre. The High Street was a steep hill with few vehicles but always busy with people. It was also very busy on the river. I would walk with my friend Billy O'Donnell to the Newcastle quayside where they had a market, selling all sorts of things to crowds of people. One day we were standing at the back of a crowd and saw a bloke being pickpocketed. We watched the thief slide his hand in a pocket and out came the wallet. We followed him around and saw him do more pockets. We should have shopped him, but we were too scared of what he might do to us.

A couple of doors up from us were two railway workers living with their mother and they had relatively good wages. "Granny Campbell" to us children, she would come to the back gate and ask one of us to go and get her a pint of beer in an off-licence, an errand for which she'd give us a penny or ha'penny. We took her tankard along and had it filled from the tap. She drank that pint at home whilst her boys went out drinking at the pub and would sometimes come home drunk.

In between us there was a house with a boy and girl whose parents were both deaf mutes, although they were fine. Another neighbour was Larry, a greengrocer who went off to war in the Middle East and was killed straight away. His wife had been just about to have a baby and she got married again.

I must have started infant school in Newcastle but I don't remember that at all. In Felling I went to Kenmire Street Primary where my teacher was Miss Cuthbertson.

Me aged about 7

We didn't have paper and pencils back then, we had a slate and slate pencil. My new teacher said to us all, in our first lesson, "Write your name out five times."

We didn't pronounce it as Ralph in the north-east. As far as I was concerned I was "Raf" (with a rolled r sound) that rhymed with chaff. So off I went on the task and I can see it now. I started in big letters at the top and the words got smaller as I worked down the slate and was running out of room:

r a f
r a f
r a f
r a f
r a f

When Miss C came along and saw my work she pulled me out from my desk and gave me a couple of belts. "That's not how you spell your name!" But of course, no one had told me how to spell it properly before that, I just spelled it like it was said. Clearly my first teacher had not been so fussy and had not picked up my error.

One day, when I was about six or so, I played truant with one of my pals as we wanted to go down to the slaughter house to watch them kill cattle. It was more difficult that we thought to sneak in as we were amazed by how many slopes and steps the animals were made to go down. Cruel, now you think about it, and a blood, messy spectacle, of course. After that we carried on down to the River Tyne to play. It felt like we had been truanting for a very long time. When we saw another boy come running down the road we thought school must be out, so we skipped off home.

It turns out we were wrong about how much time we had spent out and about. I arrived home and Mam said, "What are you doing here? You should be at school!" and as I had no good answer she gave me a belting on the bum. The next morning she took me to school and had a few words with my teacher. After my mother had departed Miss C gave me a second belting on the bottom with the strap over her desk. It bloody well hurt and I didn't miss any more school after that. She was quite a woman and a very good teacher, looking back.

We moved house again, this time to Number 17 Swards Road at the higher end of Felling. I was sent to Felling Council school where my teachers were Mr. Wilson and Mr. Nelson. I liked both of them, although Mr. Wilson regularly got on to me for always talking and I thought he punished me rather more than was necessary. A third teacher for the younger classes was Mr. Dickson who always wore a bowler hat.

Mr. Wilson happened to walk past our front door every morning on his way to work: a tall chap striding along, smart and straight. My mother was impressed by him and said, "I would like you to be a teacher one day." She never got to know that eventually I did become one.

The school was one big hall that could be divided into three classrooms with sliding partitions. One day on the other side I heard the teacher shouting at someone, saying "You're just like your brother next door!" I wondered if it was Septimus, and it certainly was. What he had done I no longer remember, but he was probably talking all the time, like I did.

Mr. Nelson was telling us about Belisha beacons, which were a new idea to make pedestrian crossings safer. He made one to show us by heating up a glass tube on a Bunsen burner, blowing a bulb onto it, and once it cooled he painted the bulb orange and made black and white stripes on the stem. Very clever, I thought.

I remember sitting next to a lad for an art lesson and we were sharing a palette with three divisions for red, blue and yellow paint. I could not put much yellow in my picture because this other boy was drinking it! That surprised me, but it didn't seem to affect him. (I thought he might come down with yellow fever, ha ha!)

We had no playing fields so we did little sport at school, and all I remember was playing cricket up against a wall.

We had a very nice childhood in Felling, spending a lot of time playing in the green spaces. I let Septimus play with me and my friends. Sep had carroty ginger hair, like sister Dorothy, and a fierce temper so we used to really fight at times. He chased me with a broom and, in trying to hit me, he smashed it onto the ground more than once. The chase went on and still he couldn't catch me, until he finally flung what was left of it at me, and he missed. Mother's broom lay in splinters across half of Felling.

Peggy with Sep and me by the gate that led to our "netty" (outside lav.) at Fieldhead

We often went up to a big grass field called The Lairies, where Sep got kicked by a horse one day. He got a stick and went up behind it and, like a fool, he tickled its bum. It lashed out and smacked him in the chest. The hooves knocked him flying and he was out cold for quite a while. It was easiest not to tell Mam anything about it.

Another time we were playing on the swings near our house and Sep was swinging up to ninety degrees, back and forth, when he slipped off the seat. He went sailing through the air and crashed onto his back and lay there, quite still, on the hard tarmacadam surface. I really thought he was dead and didn't know what to do! After what seemed a terribly long time I was hugely relieved when he came back to his senses. Again, we dare not tell our Mam, so she never knew about that either.

Other play areas were The Leam, which was a bunch of trees just outside Felling, and The Jungle which was a couple of miles to the east. There were trees to climb, ropes to swing and a stream to jump across. We would go there all day and it was lovely. Now all those pretty places are gone and the land is covered with housing.

As a boy of about eight years I was throwing stones at a glass-topped lamp post with a few other boys. They all scattered like chaff when they saw a policeman coming, but I froze! I was caught red

18

handed and got led off home by the ear where the Constable told me off in front of my mother. When he was gone my Mam smacked me hard, several times, for bringing shame to our home for all the neighbours to see.

One day Ella was helping Mam with the washing at an outhouse, which had a huge iron boiler with a door to restock the fire. Ella had opened the door and was putting more coal in when her pinafore got sucked in by the draught of the fire and she flared up in flames. Her thighs were badly burned and she carried large scars for evermore. Mam burnt her fingers to the bone helping Ella and her hands took

Peggy

months to heal. She had to go up to the Royal Victoria Infirmary regularly to get her fingers individually dressed. She couldn't even cut a piece of bread for a long time, and I had to help her with many tasks. This was awful for them both but it could have been worse.

What *was* far worse was the death of Peggy, although at the time it never really occurred to me I had lost my sister. It's funny how kids could accept that kind of thing. She was tall and skinny, with a lovely smile, and I was very fond of her.

She had left school and the only job she could get was working as a seamstress in a tightly packed workhouse in Newcastle where they made clothing. The hot, breathless and cramped conditions resulted in tuberculosis.

She ended up in Stannington Sanatorium where she died at just sixteen years old. I was too young to visit so I never saw her in the last two years of her life.

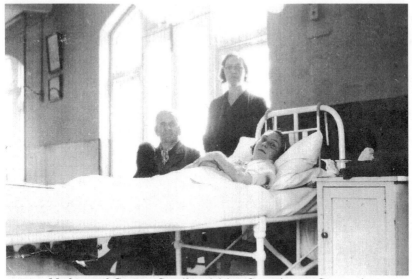

Mother and Granny Smailes visiting Stannington Sanatorium

When I joined the Air Force some years later, my chest x-ray showed a shadow on the lung. The MO asked if anyone in my family had had TB. When I said my older sister had died of it they further examined my chest and healthiness until, thankfully, they decided I was fine.

Sep and Peggy in happier days

Chapter 4
Pop Finlay and other relatives

J ohn (or Jack) Finlay, my stepfather, was nothing special and not an inspiring dad. He never took us out or did much with us, as I suppose he wasn't very interested with us not being his children. He was often drunk and was very mean with his money. Occasionally on a Saturday night he might bring a tuppenny bar of Cadbury's chocolate for us to share between three of us. That was the furthest his gift-giving usually stretched. There are only two birthday or Christmas presents I remember when I was young. One was a

quoits set which was a board with five wooden pegs on it and three rope quoits to try to throw over the pegs to get a score. The other was a bus conductor's outfit with a ticket punch.

Pop was one of many miners out of work when he met my mother. The miners were not causing trouble that I remember but in 1937 there was the Jarrow march to London to campaign for work. They came through Felling on the way to the A1 and I went to watch them come through. The line got longer and longer as people were joining them all the time, but Pop wasn't one of them. They walked every inch of the way to London, sleeping overnight on the floors of school rooms and halls.

Pop found work again in the pits at some point. He always kept his pay slip, which was a roll of tape, well to himself so Mam never knew how much he earned. He never gave her enough for housekeeping and she often complained that she was short. He'd spend money on drinking and his own interests, but very little on us. For instance, he used to go to watch the football but never took me (but then I was never really interested in watching sport anyway).

In the summer we begged mother, "Take us to the seaside!" and she would usually say she had no money, although we did manage to go a couple of times. We had to walk to the station, take the train to South Shields, then walk about two miles to the sea front. We had no buckets and spades to play with and when we finished on the beach we had to walk back again. I remember we used to walk past a rowing boat, preserved under a little shelter, which had belonged to Grace Darling, the lighthouse heroine who rescued a crew from a wreck in stormy seas.

We only ever had one family holiday, such as it was. Pop Finlay got a free holiday with the miners at Newbiggin-by-the-sea so he stayed with his pals somewhere whilst Mam, me, Sep and Ella all slept in one big room of a bed and breakfast.

Pop went off with his pals most of the time whilst Mam took us to the seaside. There was a big draughts board on the promenade that was good fun to play with Sep. The counters were made of wood with a metal band on the top so you could move them using a big pole with a hook. I remember going to the edge of the rocks, close in, and seeing the fronds of seaweed floating about. One day I was given a costume to borrow and was trying to swim when something stuck on my shoulder. It was a big jelly fish who stung me right across my back which meant I was all red spots for a week.

The miners had an athletics competition in the park that week and we went along to watch. One guy was wearing his one-piece bathing costume to throw the shot put. As he wound up for his throw his willy popped out of his swimsuit. He was only a little bloke but he had a great big willy. He didn't turn a hair, even with all the women hooting with laughter!

Pop was in his forties when he got called up to the Army for the war. He became a driver in the Royal Army Service Corps, and he ended up as a Sergeant associated with the 27th Armoured Brigade.

He sailed from Greenock and landed in Algeria where there was no permanent accommodation yet built. He slept under his lorry that first night and when he woke up he found all his kit had disappeared, including his rifle. He said he went and pinched replacement kit from others and from the stores but he often swore about "those bloody Arabs."

They were in Algeria, as part of the First Army that had to conquer Rommel's lot in Tunisia. They eventually surrounded the retreating Africa Korps, all 250,000 of them, and one of Pop's jobs was to go round taking all the weapons off the surrendered forces. This included their pocket knives of which he kept a few as souvenirs. He

eventually gave me a lovely knife - a rare and treasured gift from him - but years later I let my son borrow it and the little bugger went and lost it in the woods outside Ipswich!

Baby John, Sep, Ella and me about 1941. (Mother didn't like her picture being taken so she snipped herself off this photo.) Pop Finlay was on embarkation leave before going to North Africa and Sep is wearing his helmet and holding his Fraser Nash 303 rifle. It was quite usual to see soldiers on leave with their rifles

Pop went to Sicily and onto Italy where he got a Mention in Dispatches at Monte Cassino. His regiment was involved with rescuing some Canadian troops who were trapped on the mountainside. As a result of this they were allowed to wear the Canadian Maple Leaf on their Italian Star medal ribbon. So it seems that Pop was a war hero who was well suited to the Army. I remember him saying he loved Italy and the people, especially those who gave him extra food!

Pop's job in the pits was as a stone man who built up the roofs and sides. He had a nasty accident after the war, when part of the roof came down on him. I had come home on leave that very day and I was talking with my mother. We decided to wait up until Pop came back from the back shift which was 5 pm to 2 am. He did not turn up when expected and at about 3 am mother knew something must be wrong. She told me to go to the pit and see what had happened. There was no moon and I couldn't see a bloody thing as I traipsed across the fields. I eventually ended up at the colliery and could not find anybody. I wandered around shouting until I found a chap in the lamp cabin and said I was looking for Jack Finlay.

"Then I've got bad news for you, he's had an accident. A big stone fell on him and he is in hospital." No one from the pit had thought to come to tell Mam about it.

One of the men who had rescued him told me that a big slab of stone the size of a bed, about six feet long, a foot thick and 18 inches wide, had fallen on top of him. Fortunately, the way he was kneeling meant he wasn't flattened and killed, but the slab lacerated his back, and his chin was pushed up so that his false teeth were forced up into his nose.

Despite terrible injuries he was only in hospital for a day or two before he came home in quite a mess. There was no NHS in those days so you paid for everything you got from the Doctor, so Mam and Ella looked after him. The miners paid sixpence a week into a special fund for illness which covered him to some extent. He went back to mining for a short while before giving up work.

I went back to the old farm and visited family at times, making for very cheap summer holidays. I stayed with Dorothy, my step sister, who lived at Felton off the

Ella with Mam

Great North Road, ten miles north of Morpeth. She looked after what was left of Eshott Brocks, when it became a wartime airfield, on the other side of A1.

24

I got on very well with both her and her husband, Archie Hood. Archie was a saddler who also made and repaired the sheets that caught the corn stems cut by the reaper. These were ash rods rivetted onto thick green canvas sheets that carried the cut stems back from the reaper blade, to be pulled off the end to be tied into a sheaf. I helped with this task at harvest time. The men then took four pairs of sheaves to make into a stook which kept the grain up away from the ground. It was hard work and the stems were full of thistles, which I noticed very quickly because, unlike them, I had no gloves!

I would stay with the Hoods for a week or two. Archie set me up with a bamboo pole as a fishing rod and I went with a lad up the road who had a proper Hardy fly rod from his fisherman grandfather. We fished the River Coquet for trout. I caught one about eight inches long, but it needed to be nine inches so I had to put it back. He caught a bigger one with his proper flies and equipment. The boy had a huge lump on the side of his head, caused by encephalitis, and eventually it killed him. That was a great pity as he was a nice lad.

I liked Uncle Archie a lot, although he was short on temper and got extremely cross with me one day. The family and I were heading off across the fields to catch a bus to Alnmouth seaside. That is a beautiful place with super beaches, except you have to wade a good way out before you can swim. This meant that most folks just plodged (or paddled, as they say down south).

Archie had told me to bring the buckets and spades but in my excitement I totally forgot them. By the time we realised this we were well on the way to the bus and it was too late to go back. He was very angry that he had to buy more sand tools and I deserved his wrath.

25

Dorothy with her two boys

Uncle Archie was on the parish council, district council and was secretary for the football club and the flower club. He was a very busy bloke and a heavy smoker who always had a cigarette hanging out of his mouth. One day at a football match he just keeled over dead. When I went up to Durham University many years later, for part of my Open University course in science, I stayed with Dorothy and it was lovely to see her again.

I also went back for her funeral and it snowed like hell on that sad day.

Their son Frank was a favourite nephew. He was a farm auctioneer but he caught leukaemia and was gone in three months, poor boy, leaving his lovely wife Gillian a widow.

I went back to Fieldhead at times. Brother John was a nice chap and a good farmer. He and his wife Dora never had any children, which was a pity for them. I went to stay with them one day when they said they would take me to Linden Hall Garden Fête. Dora had prepared meat roll, a Northumberland dish of various meats (some of rather dubious origin) cooked and pressed into a roll and then allowed to cool. I was given a plate with a huge slice of what she called her speciality, and I was trying to eat this ghastly stuff and that was the hardest thing to do. It would have been easier to eat grass but I swallowed it down somehow, enthusiastically declined a second helping, and I was very sure to never eat that dish again.

We met up with my mother's brother Fred at the fête. There was a small pig given as a prize for anyone who could roll six small bowls down through six tunnels. Someone achieved it, but when they tried to pick up the pig to give to the winner, it wriggled free from their

26

arms and jumped over the fence out of the pen and ran away. My Uncle Fred ran after it and managed to catch it and he brought it back.

Uncle Fred was good at catching things! He used to poach on father's land for pheasant and fish. Whether my father knew about that, I don't know. We had a stream in a dene that ran through the farm. Fred's trick was to get a flat Haig Whisky half-bottle, put in some carbide powder and quickly fill it with water, screw it on tight and throw it in the stream where it would sink, with no air within. The calcium carbide produced gas and expanded enough to explode the bottle under the pressure. The fish got stunned and he would simply pick them off the surface into his bag.

I remember there was a plank set up for a diving board on our large pond and my Da let Mr. Moore bring the scouts from Newcastle to camp there, and they bought their milk and eggs from us.

One weekend, as a teenager, I cycled out with a couple of my friends to Fieldhead to visit John and Dora. John didn't invite us in and didn't even offer us a drink of water. He just said hello, rather vaguely, and wandered off. I had liked him very well but I found that bloody rude and a bit embarrassing in front of my thirsty friends. In his later years John bought a mattress that was water filled for comfort, but it split during the night so he woke up soaking wet. I had a good laugh, when Dorothy told me that, as it served him right!

On my mother's side I loved staying with Grandad (Andrew) and Granny (Eleanor) Smailes. Grandad was a farm labourer, horseman and cattleman. When I was seven or eight years old I had some happy days on that farm. Grandad showed me the bull held by a ring in his nose on a stick, a fierce looking brute and no doubt good at his job.

In a hole set in a thick wall lived a cockatoo, a beautiful bird with a bright yellow crest which he raised up when he was angry. Which he often was, with me at least! I poked a stick into his hole to get him to come out one day, which he duly did. He flew out and crossly bit my left ear which bled a lot, but I got no sympathy; instead I was told off for upsetting the bird.

Nearby was a railway line down which came wagons of coal. I joined in with the boys who used to very foolishly jump on the side, just above the rear wheel, and have a ride for about a mile or so, then jump off to walk back and do it again. One of the boys slipped and in trying to scramble back on the wagon he fell into the wheel which wrenched his leg off. We yelled for help and a stream of women came from the nearby cottages saying, "I knew this would happen one day, with you lads jumping on the wagons!" The boy was taken away, and I don't know how he fared in life, but we stopped that game. I went home very shortly afterwards because my holiday was over.

Grandad told me he'd only had a hobby horse before bicycles came along. Around his fireplace were five pocket watches, two of which were black-faced. Grandad had promised Sep and me we would have one each when he died. He also had a tin full of Great War cap badges which I used to play with and a cupboard full of magazines titled *War Illustrated* with lots of photos, including aircraft, which he said were destined for my collection one day.

As luck would have it, Granny died first and Grandad remarried to a very energetic lady who took in a basket of washing a day. She washed it, dried it, ironed it, all in one day, for a fee of half a crown. And so it continued for a time, until Grandad died. When we went across to see his widow, for what we thought would be a commiserating visit, we found the front door unlocked and the woman gone. Inside we found some of the old furniture but not even a piece of dishcloth remained. Everything that was not nailed down had been taken and there was not even a message left for my mother. The woman had scarpered to who knows where with all the belongings, our watches included. My mum was furious as she'd been promised linen and various other things for which she would have been very grateful.

Mam's sister, Aunty Meg, was married to an ex-soldier. Bill Wilson had been a sergeant or regimental sergeant major in a Guards Regiment; he had a deep, loud voice and we were all frightened stiff of him!

On the hill from Lowfell and Gateshead to the Tyne bridge there were long tram cars that ran up and down. One of these was driven by Uncle Bill, no doubt with military precision. He was always dressed immaculately, with boots and buttons shining, trousers pressed, and his peaked cap set dead straight on his head. Sep's first job, at age fourteen, was as a points boy on that tramline. He had a little hut to shelter in and a steel rod, like a giant screwdriver, to shoot points from one track to the other. Before Uncle Bill went up the hill he would stop at the points on the Gateshead side. He handed his enamelled tin mug to Sep which he would collect on the way back down, once Sep had filled it up with hot tea.

Meg was a housewife but at some stage I heard that she and her family were in the workhouse. I assume this was when Bill was away on active service.

Mam had another sister who played the organ at Brinkburn Priory, near Rothbury, but she died rather young and we never met.

Mam with Ella and John

*Looking after Ella and
John at South Shields*

Chapter 5
Dragged out of school

At school we took the transfer examination that later became the 11-Plus. I failed entry for the Jarrow Grammar School but got into the technical school, Jarrow Central School, in 1938. I don't remember too much about this except that I loved my science teacher, Bill Ramsey, who was an ex-World War One pilot and he soon became one of my heroes.

I had quite a lot of time off school with impetigo on my face. The clinic did the worst thing they could, which was to put a piece of plaster on it. That just made the infection creep along the plaster and spread, which meant I then needed a bigger plaster, and so it kept getting worse. People would ask. "Have you been in an accident?" I didn't really understand what it was at the time, but it was certainly messy.

My friends were Jimmy Logan, Tommy Porter and Porky Blackburn. Porky was rotund and didn't seem to mind his nickname that everyone used. In return, he called me "Rubberfoot", being just a play on my surname.

One day we came in from dinner time and were waiting for the teacher. I was having a joke wrestling match with Porky and had him spread-eagled on the desk. I suddenly realised everyone had gone quiet. We stopped and stood up, and I saw Mr. Youngson, the headmaster, who looked at me and beckoned with his forefinger. I followed him to his room where he got out a big cane, made me bend over the desk and I got four on the bottom. Gee, that hurt. It was also most unfair for just having a play fight with my friend. Porky had looked like an innocent victim at the time so he escaped getting whacked.

There were some bullies of course, like the prefects who used to wait in the cloakrooms near to whistle time and grab a couple of juniors. They would wrap up those young boys in the roller towels so they couldn't get to class or assembly in time which got them into trouble.

I went to Jarrow by train and one morning, waiting at Felling Station, I got into the only proper fist fight of my life. It was a clash of personalities. He was a stuffed shirt, a little prig of a boy with accordingly few friends. He came from a far richer family than mine, by the quality of his clothes and satchel, and it was clear that he viewed most of us as poor and ill-educated from our appearance, with shabby clothing and shoes down at heel.

I assumed he would fear my size, but he didn't. Before I knew it he whopped me a beauty in the right eye which knocked me sideways and meant I couldn't see properly. I lashed a fist back at him but, being smaller, he dodged under my blow and scarpered. Sad for me to admit, it was very clear that I had lost the fight!

I was really quite enjoying technical school when I was fourteen with two more years to go before my exams. Then, one evening my parents gave me a letter and sent me to deliver it to the education committee meeting in Jarrow and told me to wait for a reply. I handed it in and sat all evening in a chair outside the room, until eventually a man came out, quite late at night, and handed me a letter to take back to my parents.

When I got home, mother read it and said, "Oh good! They have agreed to release you early from school. We can start to look for a job for you tomorrow!" That was the whole point of taking me out, just to earn some money for the family.

In 1940 there were not many jobs, and my stepfather himself was out of work until he went off in the Army. Mam was at home. In the First World War she had been a clippy on the Newcastle buses. When the men went off to fight in the Second World War she tried to get that job back again. She could have done so but, as she had five children, she was told she should stay at home to look after her family.

I was so cross with my parents, and miserable with disappointment, knowing I would end up with no education certificate to give me any prospects. To improve my chances in life I attended evening classes after work and passed the Northern Counties 1 & 2 certificates. I greatly missed my school friends as I was never to see them again.

Chapter 6
My first employment

One of my friends was called Billy O'Donnell who attended the Catholic school opposite where we lived. We used to play in the thick bushes around the school, playing caves and hide and seek. One day in the late 1930s I came across a hoard of Cadbury's chocolate which was damp in the dew. I left it well alone, as presumably someone had pinched it and had left it there for temporary safe keeping.

Billy had a very bad chest full of asthma so he got an outside job as a window cleaner. He took time off school to do his work but every time he played truant the priest master thrashed him with a cane the next day. As he was earning half a crown or more a day Billy could put up with the thrashings.

Billy's older brother John had a paper round which he got Billy and me to deliver for him. John took the big payment for doing very little whilst Billy and I delivered them for just tuppence each. The Sunday papers were pretty thick and heavy, yet we took about seventy of these each. I had no bag and had to go up one big hill and down the other side carrying these things. So that was my very first paid job for a very small amount of pocket money.

When I had to leave school in 1940 the only job I could find was as an errand boy for the Dolcis Shoe Company in Northumberland Street, Newcastle. I rode a typical trade bike with a big carrier frame on the front to deliver shoes all over Tyneside. I loved the job and soon got to know every inch of the area and could plan my own best routes. There was one delivery at Wallsend where the house number was in the three figures; finding that for the first time was quite difficult as many of the houses had no numbers at all.

Whenever I could I would hitch a ride to save me both time and pedalling. I would come alongside a stationery or slow-moving bus or lorry, rest alongside and grab on to it. I would keep my hold as it moved and then let go once it had reached a suitable speed. I had a very nasty fright one day on the high-level bridge over the Tyne, the one with the upper deck for rail and the road underneath. I happened to get alongside a slow-moving wagon which had a three-wheeler motorised cab on the front. The trailer it towed behind had hooks around the edges for roping down the cargo. I came alongside and hung on to the trailer and I didn't realise my carrier had got snagged under one of these hooks. As he picked up speed I let go of my hold but found I couldn't get loose and was getting too fast. That was the first time in my life my heart seemed to leap up into my throat (but certainly not the last!)

I was wondering what on earth I was going to do, as I frantically tugged and heaved the handlebars sideways. Eventually my bike came unhooked about half-way along this bridge and I wobbled away from the vehicle. The episode had frightened the life out of me and I was shaking like a leaf. I never did that again!

Nearly all the girls in our shop smoked, so whenever I went out on the bike they would ask me to buy cigarettes for them. Kensitas was what they liked best, then Capstan, but these were like gold dust and if they came in to a shop they often went straight under the counter. I usually couldn't find their preference so I would have to buy whatever was available, like Craven A or Players Weights, which were cheaper and considered not to taste as nice.

I had to do other errands apart from shoe deliveries. The boss said, "I want you to take these Van Heusen collars to so-and-so shop, and you will be given a parcel to bring back to me." So off I went with these stiff, starched collars and found I was given a parcel of bananas - something we had not seen for yonks. It seemed that these shop managers swapped goods black market style.

At Dolcis we worked six days a week Monday to Saturday 8:30 am to 6 pm. Wednesday afternoon we had off for early closing, and on that day my mother always made me liver and mashed potato which I loved. On the other days I got an hour for lunch and would buy my own. I had pie and chips or pease pudding with mash in a little café for the busmen up on Haymarket Bus Station. That meal cost a shilling and if I went to the wartime Civic Restaurant for a more adequate meal - but still not really enough for a growing lad - that cost me one and thruppence.

Going to work earned me twelve shillings and sixpence a week. Out of that, it cost me sixpence a day there and back on the tram, totalling

34

three shillings. My lunches cost about 6s a week. That left me three shillings and sixpence, of which the 3s went to Mam for housekeeping and I got to keep just sixpence for pocket money. Those three shillings bought us quite a lot of stuff like eggs, bacon and butter at the Liptons shop not far from our house. (Liptons the tea merchants were general grocers at that time.) A pound of back bacon cost a shilling, but streaky was 11 pence ha'penny. Being a crafty clogs, I thought, "Aha! I can get the cheaper bacon and keep a ha'penny for myself!" But Mam, of course, saw straight away it was not back bacon so I earned a clip round the ear for cheating her out of... my own money! Naturally I didn't try that trick again.

When Pop Finlay was unemployed, and before he was called up, he joined several men who were offered the chance to build a meeting hut for the Boy's Club. In return for their labour they each got a weekly coupon for three and sixpence (3s 6d) to spend at Liptons, and that helped Mam greatly as the voucher had to go towards groceries and could not be wasted by him on beer in the pub!

Despite my hard work I had very little spending money. One day I went past the sports shop and saw some excellent roller skates in the window. I looked at them longingly for weeks but the price tag was 14s 11d and there was no way I could save that much money. Even though, one day outside that very window, I happened to look down and spotted two dropped coins, a shilling and a sixpence. I had my foot on them straight away, but it didn't sufficiently boost the coffers.

My mother used to send me up to Morpeth on the afternoon bus on Wednesday market day, which was my half-day afternoon off, to meet brother Tom. I used to love going up there as it felt like my home country, not like Felling. Tom would be in the Queen's Head pub where he gave me a cheque to take to mother, to help her manage. One day he kindly asked, "Is there anything you want for yourself?" I told him about that pair of roller skates and he wrote me out a cheque for 14s 11d as a gift from him. I was most grateful and had good use out of those skates for a couple of years.

I eventually managed to save up for a bicycle. I saw an advert in the paper for a second-hand bike for 15 shillings and had to walk nearly five miles to collect it. When I arrived I saw the tyres were totally flat. I asked the lady if I could have or at least borrow the bicycle pump, but she said they didn't have one, so I had to walk all the way home as well, pushing the damn thing!

Every night at around 5 pm it was time to wrap up the shoes that had been brought in for repair. The boss would have labelled them with what needed doing. Some special repairs I took to Boultons, the cobbler just around the corner. All the others I would wrap into a great big parcel which might be twenty pairs in a day. The boss showed me how to tie them up very well with bands of string. I would make out forms in triplicate; one was kept in the shop, the others I took with the shoes to the station. They went on the 7 o'clock train all the way to Leicester for repair. It was quite a mile or more to the station and I couldn't use the errand boy bike as it was locked up for the night and I was not entrusted with a key. I always hoped the boos would give me some tram money at least one way, to get me there with the heavy parcel, but he never did. So I had to walk all the way there and back to catch my own tram home, which departed from nowhere near the station! I was a strong lad though and hard work and long days did me no harm.

I worked as the errand boy for two years. Then I came to work in the shop, as most of the male staff had gone off to war and the boss needed someone to serve the men.

The boss was called Mr. Turner. He used to disappear for a long lunchtime every day from about 2 pm to getting on 4 pm. He possibly went to have some sort of sauna, I thought, as he came back looking very fresh. He had lost his daughter to polio when it was in its infancy here. He was very bitter, probably wondering why a scruffy beggar like me could be running around cheerfully whilst he had lost his lovely daughter. He was mean and tough and I remember his face always being black as thunder whenever he spoke to me! His wife was a nice lady, I know, as he sent me up to his home once for something. They lived in a big semi-detached house right out of the town in High Heaton. Meanwhile, my family were squeezed in a two-room flat built in the 1700s (which has long since been demolished).

There were some outstanding girls working in the shop. The three Henry sisters, two married and one younger, were great company and always up for a joke. On the other hand, Miss Barrett was a tough old girl as was Miss Bennett, the lead lady on the shop floor.

36

There was a lovely, pretty girl called Joyce who I loved to chat to. She sold children's shoes at 2s 11 ½d and 4s 11 ½d a pair. One day we were talking about kiddie's shoes when I said, "You wouldn't know, you haven't got any children."

To my surprise she said, "Yes I have, I have a little girl."

"But you are not married!"

She smiled at me, "You don't have to be married to have a baby, you know, Ralph."

At dinner times I played snooker with another lad at a billiard hall down in a nearby basement. On other days I would just walk around the shops. Grainger Street had a large covered market with an open frontage so that you could walk around all the stalls from any starting point. I used to love wandering around in there, especially near Christmas with the poultry hanging all over the place.

I remember one bizarre sale I made in our shop. We stocked a soft leather Tecnic boot from Northamptonshire, the sort the police used, and we sold them in some large sizes. A Russian sea captain came in to Dolcis for a new pair of boots as the soles were hanging off the ones he was wearing, eaten away by salt water I suppose. The biggest Tecnic boots I had in stock were size 12½. The policemen seemed huge to me but his feet were even bigger than theirs. He forced that pair of boots on and kept them on, gave me the 21 shillings and walked out, grinning with pleasure. They must have been as tight as hell but he was highly delighted!

Working in Newcastle during the war was certainly interesting. The boss said one morning, "There will be no shoes from Norwich for quite some time. I hear their factory was bombed last night." Indeed, hundreds of pairs of footwear had been destroyed.

One weekend I walked with my mate Billy O'Donnell to the quayside when the swing bridge was just beginning to swing, and we were staggered to see what was coming up the river: a U-boat! After a moment of horror we realised it had been captured and was being taken for examination at Vickers Armstrong, the big armaments company based near Elswick.

We were often getting bombed at this time. Once every eight nights I had to do fire-watching duty for Dolcis. I went to the attic with two old Jews, who always wore bowler hats and big black coats. They

37

taught me to play fives and threes at dominoes. I took along a sixpence to play with and they always took the money from me, they never let me win. I sometimes went out onto the roof to pick up shrapnel for my collection.

There was one terrible night in September 1941 when I was still an errand boy. The char lady was a lovely old girl who cleaned up our shop but she didn't come in before us one morning. The boss announced that, "Mrs ___ has lost her daughter, son-in-law and their family when a bomb hit their house last night." She came in later on that morning, gently crying to herself, which was quite heart-breaking.

On the same raid that night the New Bridge Street Goods Yard took a direct hit. This was a main distribution centre for foodstuffs for the North East. It was a huge place and months of supplies were destroyed. They included stocks of sugar, butter, margarine and other fats which meant that after they had caught well on fire the blaze burned solidly for days. The road was shut off by the police but I went nearby on my delivery round and I have never seen so many hosepipes in all my life.

The shoe shop had two staff rooms for male and female staff. There was no stock room, but above the false ceiling of the staff rooms was a considerable gap to the shop ceiling. Boxes of end-of-line men's shoes were stored up there from years before. I was selling shoes at between 15s and 21s a pair but I could see the boxes up there were marked 8s 1d and 10s 11d.

I said to the boss, "Those are good shoes up there. They will sell like hot cakes at that old price!" And they did. I got some down, getting covered with dust for my trouble, and gradually sold about half of them.

I worked for four years at Dolcis until July 1944. When I left, I arranged for Sep to come and take my place and he sold the rest of those old shoes. The boss should have been highly pleased with the Rutherford boys, but he would never say it if he was.

Chapter 7
Rockfist signs for the RAF

L ike many boys I was entertained by the weekly illustrated story books like The Champion, The Wizard, The Rover, The Skipper and Film Fun. One favourite story that sticks in the mind was the Wolf of Kabul, a British Intelligence agent on the North-West Frontier. His sidekick was an oriental who went into battle armed with a cricket bat, which he called "Clicky-Ba", with which to whack the enemy.

The best serial, for me, was Rockfist Rogan in The Champion. He was a First World War pilot who was also a boxer and shared initials with me. When I came rushing to my friends to tell them all about his latest exploits, they started calling me Rockfist, a nickname which stuck and I was quite delighted with. I also avidly read Biggles books to join the thousands of boys who dreamed of being a pilot.

Because I wanted to fly, I joined 361 Squadron of the Air Training Corps (ATC) in 1942. I worked hard and enjoyed my two years at the squadron.

My best friend there was Norman Brown, a Corporal in ATC. We worked together as a pair learning navigation, star charts and Morse code up to 24 words per minute. I spent some of my hard-earned cash on aircraft recognition books until I knew all the British and German aircraft when we were tested on them. We sat in a darkened room and one of the ATC officers would operate the flash projector to give us a split-second look at a picture of the tailplane, canopy or a bit of wing. You had to be pretty good to identify it. Our squadron came top in the North East for aircraft recognition and we were given a plaque to put up in High Felling Council School hall, which is where we had our meetings. (The Headmaster of that school was our CO.) We also met at the church hall on Holly Hill for PE and the teacher would send us off on a run up to The Leam and back, which was a wooded, grassy area about two miles away. We never got showers afterwards, we just had to cool off naturally.

There was a bright group of us who got Stage 1 & 2 Proficiencies. We were the high fliers in the Corps who tried to lead the topics back to advanced aeronautical subjects as we were so keen to be pilots. I don't know how many of the others made it. It certainly took me a long time to get my Wings.

I was made Sergeant and was in effect a Flight Commander as, although there was an older Flight Sergeant above me for which he received an additional badge, it seemed to me that I did most of the work while he stood back.

We were told that Flight Lieutenant (Flt Lt) Roderick Learoyd, VC was coming to Newcastle Town Moor one Saturday to give a speech to all the ATC squadrons. I desperately wanted to go to this special parade and asked Mr. Turner for Saturday afternoon off. He said, "Certainly not! I need you here." That Saturday lunchtime I went for a walk, as I usually did, but this particular time I didn't come back! I got a proper bollocking on Monday but it was worth it as I got to see Flt Lt Learoyd, VC. That was the only time I ever had off, in my four years at Dolcis, so Mr. Turner couldn't really grumble.

We did various weekend trips and fun activities in the ATC. We fired rifles several times and I found out I was a good shot. We also had the chance to fire a Sten gun which was excellent fun!

Twice we went to RAF Ouston for the day to be given flights in a de Havilland Dominie. The first trip was for about 35 minutes over the Lake District and it was thrilling to be in the air for the first time. It was so exciting for us youngsters to look down on the marvellous views of mountains and huge lakes from only 1,500 feet.

In contrast, the second trip was a bitter disappointment. We were going up alphabetically and, being an "R", I was one of the last to go. I can remember the CO saying, "There is just one more group," when it was five minutes to five o'clock. The pilot was looking at his watch and muttering something about his tea. Then he said, rather uncharitably, "Oh alright, I will give them a circuit," and that's what he did. We climbed in, he took off, one circuit downwind and landed again. The miserable wretch.

One day in 1943 we went up to Eshott airfield just by Eshott Brocks which had been one of my father's farms. Eshott was home to 37 OTU. It was a very murky, miserable, drizzly day, and we happened to arrive after two aircraft had collided above the airfield, possibly due to poor visibility. We were taken out to the crash site and walked around the smouldering wrecks. I saw a small metal bottle that I grabbed and pulled into my tunic to bring home. I was never quite sure what it was but I should never have taken it.

I believe one of the planes was a Typhoon from RAF Acklington, where Gerry Sayer had flown from. He was the chap who had flown the very first British jet prototype but by this time he had sadly died in a Typhoon.

In 1944 we were taken to visit RAF Milfield, home to 59 OTU specialising in ground attack, where the boys were learning to do rocketing on the Typhoons that I was so keen to fly. On the day we went they were doing practice rocketing with Tiger Moths that had rocket rails fitted. Sergeant Pepper was one of the squadron pilots who kindly showed us round and told us what they were doing. He was a real hero to us. Some of those pilots went on to attack the German tanks in the Falaise gap in the early invasion. They took a heavy toll, as by coming in low to fire rockets they were very vulnerable to being shot down.

In Spring 1944 all the tanks from up north were coming down south ready for the invasion, although we did not know why at the time, of course. The road in Northumberland Street had just been relayed with a new surface, and the tanks chewed the whole lot up! It had to be redone. They were going through all day from storage, possibly from the Army training depot at Otterburn Camp, or from Felton Park where there was a big camp in a magnificent scenic spot. I was visiting a family farm there when I watched some soldiers catch a huge salmon a yard long, as it leaped up the six steps to rise above the waterfall there, so the men had illegal fresh salmon for tea.

When I stayed with Charles in 1944 there were huge bangs coming from Redesdale ranges all day long. The exercises went over some of Charles's land and he told me that eleven soldiers were sleeping on the ground under one of his hedges when a heavy tank plunged through the hedge and killed them all.

In October 1943 I met up with one of my older ATC pals, Tommy Henderson, and we went to volunteer for the Royal Air Force at the Labour Exchange in Newcastle. Tommy was accepted, but when the man at the counter took my date of birth he told me I had to go away and come back in a month. I was not quite old enough, as I needed to be 17 and a quarter.

I returned a month later to the same recruitment office. I liked the sea, and the air, so I reasoned that if I went on an aircraft carrier I could get to see the best of both worlds. I had seen the adverts that called me to "Join the Y Scheme."

I told the recruiting officer that I wanted to go into the Fleet Air Arm but he said, "If you go on the Y scheme, it's an 18 month waiting list to be a pilot. You will only have to wait nine months in the RAF." I said, "Okay, RAF pilot then, please!" and my application was sent off.

(One of my other pals, called Lambert, did make it on the Y scheme. He only got accepted once he'd acquired contact lenses. I had never heard of the things before he got some that year.)

Eventually I received a confirmation card from the RAF but I didn't realise my boss at Dolcis would also be sent a card. The next morning at work he came up to me with a face as black as thunder, with the card in his hand. He demanded, "Does your mother know about this?" I said yes, I had volunteered to be a pilot. "Hmphhhh!" he puffed and stalked off. That was in November 1943 and he still had me in his employ until July 1944.

Tommy, who volunteered with me, wanted to be an air gunner and as they were very short of gunners he was taken in straight away to be trained on a course lasting only three months. When they were in urgent need, they shortened the courses considerably. Poor Tommy was killed before I even started. He did 11 ops and was shot down and killed on his 12th Op by the end of February '44. I heard about the loss from his mother who always met us at her gate after all our ATC meetings. This particular time she was crying and when I asked why, she told me Tommy was missing. I said, "Don't worry too much, he is probably a prisoner of war and he'll be back." But he never did come back. He was an only child, a very nice lad who was tall and good looking, but sadly he lies buried in Ibbenburen on the Ruhr.

Another older ATC friend, also from Felling, was Colin Colquhoun, a very nice chap who made Wing Commander and was decorated. He was three years older than me and was in time to be trained to join in the fighting, flying Spitfires. After the war he flew Vampires, like

42

I did later, and he was one of the six from 54 Squadron who made the very first jet flights across the Atlantic in their Vampires.

One of my school friends, John Hall from Sunderland Road in Felling, joined the merchant navy on the convoys. He was lucky to be alive to do so, as his house stood opposite a factory where they made big batteries. One morning, in about 1936, there was a huge explosion that sent a slab of stone smashing through his window onto his bed. Had he not already got up that morning he would surely have been killed. His luck did not hold out, however. He went on one convoy, came back and we had a chat, then he went off on another and I never saw him again.

Me posing with Pop's army rifle

Chapter 8
Initial training at Cannock

I n February or March of 1944 I received a rail warrant to take me to Doncaster for aptitude tests. For one of them you sat in a simulator and the lights blinked red or green, for one direction or the other, and you had to use the throttle and stick to keep the little dot in the middle of the cathode ray screen. It was quite simple but effective and I found it all a doddle.

On July 8th, 1944 I was sent to ACRC, Air Crew Reception Centre, at St John's Wood in London. I was given a service number of 3042731, with the 3-prefix signifying I was an ex-ATC boy.

Within a fortnight we were kitted out and had our inoculations... and we got paid! The first pay was 3s a day, but I sent my mother 1s of it. Of my 2s a day, I blew most of that on cherries! I had never seen them before and went barmy for them. I bought them by the pound whilst I was in London that summer!

I kept 6d away from the cherry seller which was fortunate because one morning the Corporal on parade asked me, "Do you shave yet, Cadet?"

I said, "No, Corporal."

He said, "Well you bloody well will."

I said I had no shaving gear and he said I must get some. The NAAFI had a stick of soap for a penny, a plastic-handled razor for tuppence, and three razor blades for a penny each. They had no brush in stock so I had to buy that later on. I overdid the blades, as one blade lasted me over six months with just the little fluff I had on my young chin! (Then in 1950 I bought a Philishave, one of the early Philips rotating electric razors, which I still had until recently and it still worked.)

My time in London was in the midst of the buzz bombs (V1 flying bombs) that had started on June the 13th and were raining down. The St John's Wood billet was a block of flats full of cadets. A day or two before our intake arrived a bomb had hit one side of the building. It had killed about ten cadets and when we arrived the blood-stained sheets were still hanging down from the walls. Because of this incident, instead of the cadets being spread out across the different storeys as before, we now had to have all the beds crammed together down in the basement. With a hundred cadets being packed into this basement in the middle of summer, with three-tier bunk beds only a foot apart either side, it was very hot and unpleasantly stuffy so we were glad we would only be there for two weeks.

Me in my RAF cadet pilot uniform, with the white flash in the cap signifying aircrew

The cadets were from all over the country. I didn't make any particular friends in that short time except Ginger Sharp from Bradford, Yorkshire. He was sharp both by name and by nature. We were on guard duty one night when a young woman came along the road. Ginger, sharp as ever, immediately said, "You stay here Geordie, I will take her home," and off he went. I could hear him chatting her up as they walked. When he came back, I asked how he got on and he said with a grin, "Well, I got my hand away!"

We ventured into London, of course, and for most of us it was our first visit to the capital. We wanted to go to the pictures but when we found the cost in London was about ten shillings a ticket we were shocked. We had been used to paying a shilling, or taking the cheap sixpenny or ninepenny seats, so we didn't go to the movies after all. Instead, we sat and ate delicious cherries we bought from a street barrow.

After our first week in London we started doing fire watch duty. I was at Marylebone Hospital, continually patrolling the corridors around the wards with another cadet. If an attack caused a fire we had to sound the alarm and do our best to contain it. The pair of us worked our way up through the different floors each night until we

45

were on the roof. On one night I will never forget seeing five buzz bombs come "put-put-put" across the sky with their little red tails of flame. It was a worry, as we couldn't get off the roof quickly. They all fell, but in the darkness we couldn't see where they were coming down until we saw the flash and heard the boom of the explosion.

Then one morning we were behind the hospital enjoying a cup of tea and a wad in the NAAFI which was in a little hut behind the hospital. We heard what we thought was a motorbike coming down the side of the building, but the noise suddenly stopped and someone shouted, "Get down!" We all crashed to the floor with our wads and tea going everywhere. Then, whoomph! The flying bomb landed on the other side of the hospital on the Marylebone Road Station signal box, which disappeared along with the four men inside it.

Next to the signal box had been a pile of metal shoes, used for holding down rails on the sleepers, which the explosion threw in all directions. Plenty of these embedded themselves in the hospital walls and crashed through the office windows but thankfully it was break time and the girls were not at their desks. That whole episode frightened the life out of us.

After finishing in London our intake of cadet pilots U/T (Under Training) was sent to Cannock County Mining College for six months of Pre Air Crew Training (PACT) where we were split into four flights of 25 cadets.

We had PT and fitness on two or three days a week, a little square bashing, but mainly classroom education in English, physics, geography, history and airmanship. The physics tutor happened to be a maths genius who could easily multiply two four-digit numbers in his head.

We had Saturday and Sunday off as the college was closed for the weekend except for the canteen that was open for our meals every day. The principal, Dickie Payne, was a lovely old boy who always seemed to be there. He set up a special room with beds in so that cadets could come back and visit as he just loved their company. After we left Cannock a pal and I went back a couple of times to stay with Dickie when we had nothing else to do.

We ate all our meals at college but stayed in a local billet. Mine was a civilian billet in Wolverhampton Road with Mr. and Mrs. Poole.

The other chap staying with me was Brian "Woody" Woodfield who came from Winchmore Hill in London. Both his parents had committed suicide but I didn't hear why. He was actually a bit weird himself but we got on well enough. Except when he peed in my boot one night! He had been out drinking and couldn't be bothered to go down to the toilet, so he picked up a boot to piss in, and it happened to be mine. I had to pour it out of the window in the morning and then had to put up with a damp sock all day, the bugger.

We didn't have enough money to go drinking very much. I was never really a drinker and half a pint of shandy is really pushing the boat out for me, these days.

Mr. Poole was always ill with a stomach ulcer. As we had no meals at the billet we only saw the householders for a few minutes at either end of the day. The Pooles went out and left us alone one night and Woody and I decided to let their budgerigar out to have a fly around. Then we found we couldn't get the bugger back in his cage until eventually we totally ignored him, at which point he went back on his own. That was a relief as there would have been hell to pay if he had still been fluttering about when they got home!

A third friend of ours was George Stansfield. He and Woody were closer as they had no girlfriends and so they hung around together when I was out with mine.

Cannock Chase is a delightful place where everyone took their girlfriends for a walk. I had been in love with a girl who lived opposite our house in Felling, but I only saw her through the window and we never actually met. My first girlfriend was a local girl from Cannock called May Hollingshead, who was in service at a big house which was a shop as well. I asked her out and we went to the pictures once or twice and to a dance a couple of times, but otherwise we would just walk out up on the Chase or visit her family home. I got to know her Dad who was a miner and her brother who was a welder making drop tanks for fighters.

Cannock U/T intake 1944

Back row:

1. B Wilcock 2. C Tuffnell (Essex) 3. Williamson
4. J Tweddle (Geordie) 5. David Shepherd 6. P W Topping

Middle row:

1. David Reid 2. Brian "Woody" Woodfield 3. George Stansfield (Colwyn Bay)
4. Charlie H Walker 5. RR "Ginger" Sharp 6. E Armstrong (Kettering)
7. J H Stevens (The Dancer) 8. J Higgen (The Undertaker, Hull)
9. David Whiting 10. E Wells (York)

Bottom row:

1. W Richardson (Gateshead) 2. L Rothery (Yorks.) 3. G White (Worcs.)
4. P/O Busby
5. J "Tibs" Theobald 6. D A Taylor (Hove) 7. Yours Truly

Note: These names as I recall them over 70 years on, with apologies if any are incorrect.

The back of my photo signed by AH Baker and F Hood but I don't think they are in the picture. David Whiting is a name I was fairly sure of, but had not signed the picture, so I could be wrong. Please contact the publisher if you can correct me or if any survivors or relatives wish to get in contact.

49

May and I parted ways after a while and I walked out with another
girl from the little town of Rugely. Her father asked if I would like to
go down the pit to see what a miner gets up to. We went down the lift
and then took a long walk along the rail tracks from the bottom of the
shaft to the coal face. We started off standing but the height gradually
decreased as we went along, until I was horrified to find we were
crawling to work in only about a yard of height at the coal face. He
said, "There you are, fill me a bucket of coal!" I hacked and hacked
and even after a long time trying I am not sure I ever did fill that
bucket. When I saw what my stepfather Pop was actually involved
with as a miner I was quite horrified and said to myself I would never
work down here in a thousand years.

There was one shameful episode at Cannock. P/O Busby was the CO of the squadron, a nice chap and a good boss. When we had been packed in the basement in St Johns Wood I had found a fountain pen on the floor. I tucked it in my pocket and used it as my own.

One day I got called in to Busby's office to find another cadet from a different flight was already in there. Busby asked me, "Do you have a fountain pen, Cadet?"

I said that I did, and he said, "Please let me see it."

I presented it from my pocket, and he asked the lad, "Is this the one?"

"Yes, Sir"

Busby carried on to me, "Where did you get it?"

"My Grandmother gave it to me," I lied, being the first thing that came into my head.

"Are you sure you are telling the truth, Rutherford?"

I could feel my face getting redder and redder and knew I was caught. He very well knew it too, as he said, "I don't think so, and I think we will return it to its rightful owner."

I handed it over and was very fortunate that nothing more was said. Naturally, I should have tried to find the owner when I first found it, but I had never had a fountain pen and like a fool I wanted it. I still feel guilty about that, 75 years later.

One of the lads called Stevens (but not my great pal Steve) bought a book by Victor Silvester, a chap who helped make ball room dancing popular. It had diagrams of all the footmarks and how to do the steps. We tried this out and it worked! I had only really hopped around before that time but now I could dance a little.

Higgen had worked for an undertaker in Yorkshire and he told me that when they came to a body where rigor mortis had set in, his job was to use the mallet and make sure the limbs would go in the coffin!

At the end of my course I got a certificate, the equivalent of a GCE, and I had good passes in all subjects. When I went to Cannock I couldn't swim, but Sergeant Scully got us up to Bronze Medal Life Saving standard. Because the war was on I didn't get a medal, I just got a little card. I still carry that in my wallet, although these days I somehow think the sight of me diving in would not inspire very much hope in a drowning soul!

In January 1945 we were sent to Torquay for a second set of aptitude tests. These tests were much more involved and took all week with tests and puzzles, like a diagram of cogs asking, "If wheel C turns clockwise, what direction will wheel Z turn?" Again, I didn't have any difficulty with them, or so I thought.

I remember marching up and down the seafront where we could see the tail of a Focke-Wulf 190 sticking up out on the shoreline.

At the end of the week in Torquay we all lined up in the Grand Hotel waiting for the results to come up on the board. Only a few people got what they wanted, and I wasn't one of them. It turns out they had plenty of trained pilots coming through from Rhodesia and Canada to carry on, so of our hundred U/T they only kept nine. They kept 37 others as suitable for air gunners, and I was unfortunately only one of those. The rest were all made redundant and many were sent to become army paratroopers.

The Navy had the top of the six or seven floors in the hotel. The funny thing is they could not leave the hotel without the permission of their Chief Petty Officer. They had to wait for a liberty boat, as they can't leave a ship otherwise. Even on dry land they could not leave the "ship" until the CPO said the next liberty boat was leaving! Seemed crazy, but despite that I still would have liked to slide across and join them. One chap had failed to pass the tests to become a pilot in the Fleet Air Arm that he wanted so badly, and was so upset that he went to the top of the hotel and jumped off to his death.

I still had a very strong Northumberland accent at this time. Some people didn't understand me at all, and I had trouble with a variety of other people's accents. I could understand the ones who, unlike me, spoke the King's English. Not many people I met spoke really "posh" in the RAF, just normal and reasonable accents. I had to totally change my speech over the years. I preferred Rockfist, but I was inevitably called Geordie, in the same way as nearly all the Scots were called Jock and the Welshmen were all Taffy.

I never saw Woody again after the course until a few years ago when I spotted him in a picture with 36 Squadron and a Mosquito in *Flypast* Magazine. And one of the officers in that picture I also recognised as he had lived two doors up the road from us in Swards Road, Felling. I wish I could remember names like I recognise faces.

Chapter 9

Held at Bridgnorth

Instead of being trained as pilots, or even air gunners, we were posted to RAF Bridgnorth holding unit. (I went to Bridgnorth three times in all, but shan't single out the separate visits.)

At Torquay I had made a new friend who became a good chum when he ended up at Bridgnorth with me. He was the same intake as me, at another PACT centre at Salford whilst I was at Cannock. Arthur Stevens, who I always called Steve, was a Cornishman from Fowey between Truro and Plymouth. His mother lived in Plymouth but he lived with his grandparents at Fowey as he liked it there. He got engaged to a Fowey girl, but she broke it off and sent the ring back. We spent ages visiting all the jewellers we could in the hope of finding one who would buy it back from him, but nobody would!

RAF Bridgnorth was not exciting. We had drill every morning, lessons in admin and RAF law, and were on guard duty quite a few nights on the RAF station although there was no operational runway there. We tried to liven things up by larking about and got into a bit of trouble at times.

Steve and I heard that in the corner of the station one of the big wire panels in the fence had a loose bottom, so if you pushed it up you could get out and avoid the guard room. We went across the fields to a pub to buy a pint of cider and we met a couple of girls to spend the evening with. We returned after midnight and as we came under the wire we heard the patrol dogs barking. We started running like hell across the grass to the huts. What I didn't see in the dark was a manhole cover that had been left open, so one leg went straight down and I smashed down onto my face and practically knocked myself out. I was dazed but I got up and ran on to the hut and jumped into my bunk fully clothed, panting like mad. It was a crazy jaunt but somehow nothing was broken and we didn't get caught.

Another time Steve and I were letting off a bit of steam, having a bit of a pillow fight and wrestling to burn off some energy. Steve suddenly dashed out of the hut and he flung the door open, which slammed back and cut my hand (and I still have a scar there) so I flung my pillow round the corner to hit him. Just my luck that our Corporal, Wally Roper from Liverpool, came in at that very moment and the pillow hit him plumb on the nose. I got jankers for that in the form of cleaning showers and toilets.

That wasn't the only pillow fight incident. I was pressing my best blue uniform in the bedding store when Steve attacked me. I started whacking him back without realising a pillow had knocked the iron over onto the trouser legs and was merrily burning through them. Fortunately an ex-operational air gunner in charge of the stores saw my plight. He arranged for his chum in the clothing store to snitch me a new pair. Hurrah for the ex-Ops boys! Most of the ones I knew were great.

Arthur "Steve" Stevens. One of my best pals from Cornwall

One weekend Steve and I were alone in the hut, playing cards, as it was too far away for us to go home for the weekend, unlike many of the others. Around came the padre, who was sporting an AG wing having flown Ops on Bostons. He chatted to us and persuaded us to come to his office and start confirmation classes, as neither of us had been confirmed. We went to those for four weeks until he said we were ready to go to Ludlow to be confirmed by the Bishop. On the night before that, he wanted us to confess, although I couldn't think of anything I needed to confess about, myself. Anyway, I was called into the office first and I had to kneel down in front of him, and as I did so, he moved round behind me and I could feel his fingers tickling the back of my head. I thought what the hell is this? So I shook my head and said, "No, no, no."

He said to send in Stevens and I went out and warned Steve to watch out. He received the same treatment, and so we reckoned the padre was a poof and we stayed away from him after that. We did get the transport down to Ludlow Cathedral to see Bishop Edmund Sara. I have never forgotten him, standing up in the pulpit, holding his bishop's staff on one side, and moving his leg on the other side, back and forth all the time in some sort of twitch, we supposed. We were confirmed and that was that, but I never became a church goer.

Another great pal of mine was Ronnie "Jock" Queen from Aberdeen. On the station were some Turkish Airforce officers who were being trained in ground studies prior to flying. They were buggers for chasing the WAAFs. (We didn't seriously chat up the WAAFS ourselves. We were just young cadets and the WAAFs weren't interested in us at all, as we didn't have much spare time nor the means to wine and dine them!)

We had to guard the WAAF quarters to prevent any unwanted visitations in the night and were on the 4 to 6 am shift. We stood out there and it was freezing bloody cold. I said, "Ronnie, there's an empty hut here. Let's go and warm up. We can watch just as well from in there." We went in and found there were some wire beds, although no mattresses, and we each sat on a bed and eventually got tempted to lay down and both nodded off. After 6 am, Wally Roper was wondering why we hadn't come back from duty. He found us fast asleep and he was hopping mad. He said, "Right, for the rest of your time here you will wash the ablutions and clean the toilets!" That was a whole month we had to do this. Wally was a good old sort though and we deserved all the punishments he gave us.

We had a go at clay pigeon shooting with our PE instructor. He walked a group of fifteen of us to the range and asked if we were all game to put a shilling in for a competition to see who gets the highest

55

score and wins the kitty. We all agreed. There were six clay trap stations, from easy to increasingly hard. At the end of that there were two of us equal without a single miss. He got us to do a walk-in to the last trap as they come straight overhead and the two of us both hit them and we walked in further, until we were so close that he missed but I didn't. I had never shot clays before and yet I hit every single one and was 14 shillings richer.

THE ROYAL LIFE SAVING SOCIETY

BRONZE MEDALLION STANDARD

POCKET CERTIFICATE

Awarded to

RALPH RUTHERFORD

R.A.F. Cannock

For Practical Knowledge of Rescue, Releasing oneself from the Clutch of the Drowning and for Ability to render aid in Resuscitating the Apparently Drowned.

Chairman of the Central Executive.   *Chief Secretary.*

Date January, 1945.

Chapter 10
Bombing up at Fiskerton

A fter about six weeks holding at Bridgnorth there was still no Air Gunnery course available, and instead I was posted out to RAF Fiskerton, a few miles east of Lincoln, home to 49 and 576 Lancaster Squadrons. I was quite pleased about that as my hero, Learoyd VC, had flown with 49 Squadron. Fiskerton was equipped with FIDO (Fog Investigation and Dispersal Operation) which was quite a sight when they set fire to the troughs. It certainly worked well in lifting the fog to clear the runway.

I was not trained for anything specifically useful by this stage so I became ground crew and was assigned to the bomb dump. The guy I worked for was Norman Brown, a nice chap, the son of a florist from Southport (and no connection to the Norman Brown who was my friend in the ATC). Norman had been out in the Middle East for a couple of years and told me that they were given a pint of water a day in the desert: you could either drink it or wash with it, your choice.

Norman said, "Geordie, we want you to drive the bombs out, once we have fused them and loaded them on the trollies." Fine I said, I didn't mind, just glad to be busy with whatever they wanted me to do. He showed me how to drive the David Brown tractor which was so easy that I picked it up in about five minutes.

In one bomb dump they still had a stock of 25-pound bombs that were over twenty years old. Norman said to me "Careful what you are doing with those ones, the explosive would have crystallised. Just one little tap and they may go up." I was rather nervous about the whole idea of handling bombs already and that little pep talk made me far worse! I was afraid to touch the damn things. But after a while I saw him chopping kindling wood for the fire on a modern bomb full of RDX, just to save bending down! Before long I was doing the same and I just avoided those old ones like everyone else.

Norman said I would need to get a licence to drive the tractor on the road so I could go out to Reepham railway station to get bombs off the train. (Fiskerton railway station was actually further away and on the wrong side of the River Witham, with only a foot ferry to get across.) The W/O arranged for me to go to the Motor Transport section to have a driving test. He said. "Off you go in your tractor to the MT section, and you'll meet Sgt Frost who will give you your test". I went over and found the Sergeant who was not a happy type, in fact he looked just like the actor Wallace Beery with an angry-looking, mangled face!

I said, "Sgt Frost, I have come over here for a driving test on my tractor." He growled something, took me outside, and told me to get on his tractor. Straight away I noticed a major difference. My tractor had a foot clutch like a car, whilst his had a hand change that I had never seen before. I told him I didn't know how to drive one like that, and could I not use my own tractor? He said there was nothing to it and showed me how to pull out the lever, change the gear, then push the lever back. Very clumsy and awkward, but not rocket science.

"Off you go," he said, and I started the test. I pulled the lever out, grabbed the gearstick to put it in gear, and pulled the gear lever right out of its socket! I felt like laughing about the mishap until I saw his face. He growled at me in a very menacing voice, "Go away! Come back in a week!" Frost by name, frost by nature. I returned with great trepidation the following week. All went like clockwork this time as he allowed me to use my own tractor, rather than break one of his, and I passed my driving test.

The other tractor driver with me at the dump was Pat Yeo from Cornwall. As well as the tractor I had to drive a huge Coles finger truck (or forklift). I sat pretty high up on the seat, had a wheel with a handle on it, and a big hydraulic lift with arms sticking out the front. I got good at turning it very quickly, although one day I overdid it and managed to tip it over onto the cinder pathway.

There were two main types of bomb that we handled. The first were 1,000lb bombs that looked like a traditional bomb with a rounded nose and a tail fin. Then there were the 4,000lb bombs called cookies which were just delivered as a cylinder, like a big oil drum on its side.

Some of these were delivered by lorry and were offloaded directly into the dump, and others came by train. Reepham Station was less than half a mile away and I would run around the peri-track and collect a 4,000 lb bomb from the wagons with my forklift, tilt it back gently and trundle on back to the dump.

Sometimes I had to take the tractor and trailer to the station. Once in August holiday time I got to the village and there were kids milling around, and one cheeky lad said, "Give us a lift, mister!" And like a fool I stopped and gave them a ride around the village and dropped them off again. They enjoyed it but I realised it was too risky if one fell off the trailer, so I didn't do that again.

There was an abandoned farm at the end of the runway with an orchard. The airfield took away a lot of the land, I suppose, and the farmer had to pack up. In the autumn when I drove past I would stop and do some scrumping. I didn't see anyone picking the apples other than me and it seemed a shame to waste all this fruit so I took armfuls back to share.

The bomb dump had several shallow wooden ramps with a higher, flat concrete base at the start. I would bring a big bomb on the finger truck and place it on the top. A big loop of thick rope was laid on the ramp and this was used to control the descent of the bomb down the wooden ramp. I worked at the high end and a couple of blokes worked at the lower end. One day I didn't realise that I was standing inside the loop of the rope, and when it came up as the bomb rolled down, the loop caught behind my neck and trapped me. It would have broken my neck if Norman hadn't heard me yell, and he quickly got a big batten (which was half a length of railway sleeper) and threw it in front of the bomb to stop it rolling. He surely saved my life.

The bombs would be rolled down into place and then left on the racks. When they were needed they would be rolled off the low end where they were jiggled to be the right way up on a trolley and chocked to keep them still.

Once they were loaded on the trailer, one of the jobs I had to do for cookies was to fit two metal lugs on the top with four big bolts screwed into pre-tapped holes, which provided the means for the bomb to be hung in the aeroplane. Around the nose end we fitted a metal band, about six inches wide and sticking out a few inches, and screwed that on tight. On the other end we fitted a cylinder like a dustbin and screwed that on. The big bin made the tail end lighter so that the cookie fell the right way up. We then towed the bombs across to the fusing bay where the fusers would take out the blanking plug and put in the live fuse.

A cookie was set up so that when it neared the ground the air pressure, trapped by the metal nose band, would force a diaphragm to trigger the fuse. That ignited three small charges, which would cause it to explode above the ground to give an outward blast. The 4,000, 8,000 and 12,000lb bombs were made specially to blast buildings down, which they did all too well.

It took quite a while to put all these attachments on and it was a full-time job for the armourers to get all the bombs prepared when they were needed. When there was a full pelt on, everyone was mucking in to help.

After they were fused I would drive them round in my Davy Brown tractor from the bomb dump, round the peri-track and over to the Lancasters to be loaded up.

I had an incident in winter time, early 1945, when I had a long line of 1,000lb bombs on trollies. I had a lamp on the back of the tractor I could shine along the train of bombs, and I realised why I needed it that night. As I came round the bend I could see in the lamplight that the tails were shaking in the air, which meant the noses must be down. I stopped and went back to check. It seems the chocks had worked loose over one rather uneven section of the peri track and had moved on their trollies. The heavier ends had slipped forward, and the noses had been rubbing on the ground and had got red hot! I unhooked the trollies and drove my tractor full-pelt round to the W/O and told him about this, and he came to have a look. We chocked them up as best we could, then he told me to hook the trollies on and take them round to the firing range, further on round the three-mile peri-track, to leave them there to cool off. I was afraid they might go up at any time and it was all rather alarming.

It was an important job I was doing, as were all the ground staff, but I was known to remark at times that, "I did not join the RAF to fly a bloody tractor!"

When I came on duty at 8 am, and cycled around the perimeter track to the bomb dump, I always looked to see which dispersals were empty from the raid of the previous night and my heart would sink if it was one where I'd got to know the crew.

While I as at Fiskerton I met a lovely WAAF called Carol Harding, and we used to go to different entertainments together. We went into

Lincoln to the big NAAFI clubs where you could get a good meal and dance - in fact that's where we met, at one of those dances - and she taught me a little more about dancing. We both loved Lincoln and walked around to see different places like the Cathedral and the old prison.

She was already engaged to a Canadian corporal, in 4 Group in Yorkshire, but she got posted down to Lincoln. I never even kissed her, she was just a wonderful companion in a lovely friendship.

When returning in the evening there were no buses out to Fiskerton, so we had to get a train to Fiskerton, known as Five Mile House railway station. The LNER railway ran just south of the River Witham, and the village and airfield was to the North, so there was a manually operated foot ferry to get across the river.

We got on the train one night and we had a valid ticket, but a lot of chaps didn't have. Instead they had old razor blades covered in paper, hoping the collector wouldn't see what he was taking in, as we were still in black-out conditions.

From the station we had to walk to the river crossing and go on a chain bridge, where the big wooden platform was pulled across on a chain loop. It would carry quite a few people at once. The people with dodgy tickets thrust them in the conductor's hands and rushed off, and they ran ahead and leapt on to it and tried to get over in case their fraud was found out. Some used to run and jump the last few feet to try to get on it, but someone missed it that night and ended up in the river, which was rather comical.

I can remember swimming in that river when it was hot in the summer, after the war was over, and I tried diving off that bridge. My arms went straight into the soft mud and frightened me as I got stuck for a moment, and I didn't dive again.

There was a terrible flying accident that I saw one morning. A Lancaster came flying over as I was chugging around the peri-track on my tractor. He was only at about 500 feet and I thought to myself that's a bit low. Then suddenly the nose dropped and it came down into the clothing store, where my Carol worked. I couldn't get round there quick enough, and the place was ablaze, but it was not her part of the store and she was fine.

61

There were eleven bodies from the plane, instead of seven, so they had a roll call throughout the station, and found there were twenty people AWOL. On an operational station it was easy to go missing for a bit, and have people cover for you. Once that was all sorted out, it was decided that the inexperienced crew had been flying with four extra screened crew, men with a lot of operations who were training the youngsters.

There were other crashes when I was there. One Lanc crashed on taking off at night when departing for a food parcel drop in Holland on the last day of the war. I only found out in the morning as I had finished my duties and after bombing up I would cycle round the peri track and head off home before the aircraft were dispersed. We lived a mile and a half away down a country lane in Nissen huts at No. 12 site, well away from the airfield.

Carol was demobbed as soon as the war finished and went to join her husband. She came from Prestatyn, in North Wales, and I remember thinking it was funny that the name of her house was named something very similar to Mairzy Doats, as in the popular nonsense song that was all the rage.

[We could not obtain permission to reproduce the song lyrics, although they are on the internet, which were inspired by an English nursery rhyme. One of the writers heard, "Cowzy tweet and sowzy tweet and liddle sharksy doisters" (cows eat wheat and sows eat wheat and little sharks eat oysters) and that led to this song in which mares eat oats.]

On May the 8th 1945, Pat and I went to the Motor Transport section to have the oil changed in our tractors. The sump plugs had been removed and drained when over the tannoy system came the station commander saying the war in Europe is over and everyone can stand down for the rest of the day as a holiday.

"Yippee!" we cried together, and promptly put the old oil back into the engines and set off in the drizzly rain, racing each other around the perimeter track! Elation was rife as everybody was deliriously happy, of course.

That evening I cycled into the city of Lincoln and after a cup of tea and wad in the NAAFI Club I wandered into the centre of town where it seemed every pub was full of bomber crews already well-sozzled. You couldn't blame them as they'd been to hell and back but now it was all over. After I'd quaffed a glass of ale a lady invited me and three others, who I had never met before any more than she had, to come back to her home to drink some more. I'd already had enough, being only 18 and trying to avoid too many drinks as I still had to ride my bike back to Fiskerton on a black road. (There were still no lights so soon after the hostilities and few houses along the way.)

I went off with a drunken navigator who was determined to share my bicycle but didn't really know where he was going. He insisted on riding my bike with me perched on the crossbar. When he realised I was having to return to a different station he let me go off and I half-walked and half-rode my cycle home to my quarters. That was the end of VE Day.

The crews at Fiskerton were mainly Australians, New Zealanders and Rhodesians and a few British, and they seemed hairy scary types. Next morning on May 9th they started what we called "Cooks Tours" (as in the travel agent, Thomas Cook) for groundcrew. I was amazed at how few groundcrew would risk going up in the Lancaster. I jumped at the chance and got one of the very first trips with a crew from 576 Squadron. There we were, flying at just 1,000 feet over the Belgian Uplands and into Germany the day after the war finished. We flew over Achen and Wesel where our troops had crossed the Rhine. We hardly saw any building that remained standing over three feet high and we could see the tank tracks coming in from all directions. We flew over Cologne cathedral, and how amazing it was to see it just standing there in all that space with almost everything else flattened around. The crews wanted to have a good look at it all, as having been flying so high up, only at night, they had never really seen the ground before. They were cock-a-hoop flying so low over the conquered land with no flak or fighters to worry about.

Over the high wooded area of the Ardennes we flew over several smouldering aircraft that had been shot down only a day or two before. Those night fighters were everywhere when the boys were bombing. Then we turned over the Ruhr and many more ruins and came home. I felt so proud of these chaps and the brave job they had done, and very grateful for my trip over Germany.

My work at Fiskerton continued for another five months. We were still dropping bombs - only now it was in the sea as we had to empty the bomb dump. So even after the Germans surrendered, the lads were still bombing up and dropping them in the Atlantic Ocean. I was driving bombs until about October, making eleven months at Fiskerton in all.

My next stop was at 16 MU (Maintenance Unit) at RAF Stafford, a horrible place. They were getting rid of all the equipment - engines, wings, guns, ammunition, batteries, tools, the lot. It was a terrible shame to see complete Liberator wings on the ground and a steam roller running over them and flattening them out for scrap. Many items were being dumped down a disused mine shaft in Staffordshire. Some clever boys from London got to hear about this and they were coming along, climbing in the mine, getting the stuff out and selling it. To stop this, the RAF changed their system but I am not sure of the details.

Throwing all these items away didn't make any sense. Why didn't they sell these things, or at least recycle all the metal? And why on earth did they worry about people pilfering things that were being destroyed anyway? Your guess is as good as mine. I thought some of the Pratt and Whitney tools looked pretty useful, so I pinched a couple of ratchet spanners and a set of the nut heads that fitted in them and popped them in my wellies. As we walked out of the site that evening we found the RAF Police were searching people at random. I thought "Oh Christ!" but I got through. I made great use of those brilliant tools for many years; they were far too good to be chucked down an old mine shaft.

In a short stay at Bridgnorth I caught up with my pal Steve again. When we were sent to help shut down Halfpenny Green airfield, about ten miles away, we found a Very flare gun and one red cartridge in an empty hut. We decided to fire it into the stove in the centre of the room. Well, that wasn't the best idea. The roar of the gun and oceans of red smoke that billowed out of every conceivable hole, crack, door and window of the hut was probably rather noticeable. We dropped the gun and scarpered guiltily until we were well in the clear and then breathed a huge sigh of relief.

Chapter 11
Isle of Man Air Gunnery school

I n May 1946, at long last, I was posted to RAF Andreas near Ramsey on the Isle of Man to train as an Air Gunner at No 11 Air Gunnery School. We did all the usual things and finished our training operating the guns in Wellington bombers.

I borrowed my mother's Brownie box camera for one stint on the island which means I have rather more photos, although few with me in them as I was behind it rather than in front, of course. How I wish I had been able to buy my own camera long before that and taken some of Fiskerton. (Mind you, if you were caught with a camera on any Operational Airfield you would be in trouble.)

One of our Wellingtons

I liked the island and its people. The local church had a little stall for tea and coffee where young airmen used to congregate. It was there that I met Joan Godfrey who also played organ in the church. Joan lived in Ramsey one street behind the seafront. The big waves of very stormy seas came right over the top and landed at their front door, at times.

I asked Joan out for a walk and she took me to Sulby Glen and Glen Auldyn up the mountain which had a small lake at the top with a waterfall feeding it. We went up at Easter time when the water was beautifully clear on a lovely sunny day. We had taken our costumes so I dived in but couldn't get out quick enough as it was bloody freezing! The waterfall often froze in cold winters to make an awe-inspiring curtain of hanging icicles.

Joan was a lovely girl with a swarthy skin. I asked her one day why her family had got darker skins and she said they were of Spanish descent. After Drake defeated the Armada the Spaniards scattered in all directions and, of those who went up into the Irish Sea, one galleon was wrecked on the rocky coastline of the island and some of the crew stayed there.

Joan's father was a lifeboat man. She taught me to fish one night out in Ramsey harbour in a little rowing boat where we caught 28 whiting in half an hour. I asked what we would do with them and she said, "My Dad will deal with them alright." I never got to taste one!

Joan knew all about the Isle of Man races and knew many of the Tourist Trophy riders. One rider she named was Jimmy Guthrie and there is a spot on the mountain road named after him for some incident I can't recall. We walked up to watch the bikes almost brushing the wall on the hairpin bend out of Ramsey.

Joan's brother Eddie had a new Triumph 350cc, a thing of beauty, on which he took me round the TT mountain course at a frightening speed although he was a very good rider. It was very cold and I felt frozen up on the Snaefell mountain in only my RAF battledress blouse, with no gloves or hat. Snaefell is 2,034 ft high and lots of aircraft crashed into it although I never got up to the top to see them. Planes used to fly at a standard 2,000ft wherever they were which meant that flying in stuffed cloud was the undoing of many. The same problems occurred on The Cheviot, near my home in Northumberland, which is also just above 2,000ft.

66

After leaving Douglas at the start of the TT course one comes to Braddan bridge where one has to salute the Little People or come to grief. We partook of this ancient tradition and it seemed to work for us that day.

We were haring along at Sulby Bridge, where the road does a right bend over a bridge and then a left, which Eddie took at great speed and we leapt in the air. We landed on the wrong side of the road and we could see a white sports car coming towards us like the clappers! I thought that was it for us, but the driver was also on his wrong side of the road which meant we passed each other safely! Phew! Eddie offered to take me round again sometime, but it's funny how I always seemed to be too busy. I never became a motorcyclist.

I visited Douglas, the capital of the island, a few times where they still had horse-drawn trams on the main streets. The first time I went there with a pal we were walking along the dockside past a Royal Navy ship when an angry voice came down from above, "Salute the quarter deck!" Where the hell is that, we wondered as we peered around. "I'm up here!" came a voice, which we could now see belonged to a three-stripe Commander. So, we shrugged and saluted him to make him feel better. We didn't know anything of Navy customs.

Three of us went out in a rowing boat in the harbour for something to do. I had done rowing once before on the River Severn with my pal Steve, who was a very good rower from having lived on the Cornish coast. I was rowing in Douglas Harbour when I lost my footing on the pulling stroke and managed to drop one oar and saw it go floating away. We paddled around and finally managed to collect it and no doubt the local fishermen were quietly laughing at us.

My office in the Wellington and some of my course mates (Smacky second left)

67

One of our training Wellingtons and an AOC's inspection, below

An ATC visitor, myself, Gordon "Smacky" Blease from Walton-on-the-Naze who is still ticking along, and two other chaps I can't recall

I got my Air Gunner's Wing, and I finished top of my course, and we were given some leave.

Some of my pals doing a Mr. Chad impression! (We really needed bigger noses!) Smacky is second left with Frank Williams, the son of a Group Captain, behind.

Mr. Chad was the cartoon graffiti that appeared everywhere, and merged over time with the US Forces' "Kilroy was 'ere"

Going on leave on the Steam Packet Ferry with Frankie Crook and an instructor

Frankie Crook in the picture was from Felling, same as me. After he left the RAF he became a typewriter mechanic and was out travelling when he knocked down an old lady and killed her. My sister Ella read about that in the local paper and informed me.

When we got back from leave we found lovely RAF Andreas station had been closed down as we had been on the last AG course. We were sent on to nearby RAF Jurby which was very much a peace time station: lots of discipline and not much fun. I was delayed there for a further six months whilst waiting for my first crew posting to a squadron.

On arrival at Jurby we were told, "You'll eat in the airmen's mess as you are only Air Gunner 4" (that's equivalent to a Corporal). We eventually gained a bit more respect and acceptance once we were drafted in to do various useful jobs on the station.

I spent a month in the Central Registry, which was sort of a Station Post Office, helping an ex-ops Sergeant Air Gunner, Irishman Paddy Conn DFM, to process the mail with a young admin clerk.

At Ramsey there was a POW camp and, although the war was well over, they were not yet repatriated by this time. Gunter Horst Heinz Starost had been a German paratrooper and worked as a cleaner in the central registry. I got to know him and found him to be a very nice bloke. One day he asked if I played table tennis. I said that I did, and when I asked where we could play he said there was a table in his camp.

POW Gunter, another Central Registry staff member,
fellow A/G Cab Calloway and myself at RAF Jurby 1946

I went over to the camp one evening and as I walked in I encountered the boss, Willi. He was the stereotype of an Aryan, being blond, tall and good looking and if looks could kill I would have been cut to pieces. He didn't like me being there one bit and I think Gunter got into trouble over my visit.

Gunter beat me hands down whilst the other POWs laughed at me and clapped him, but I had enjoyed the game. I was totally out of practice as the last time I had played regularly was a couple of times a week after school, back at the Boys Club in Felling (the one that my stepfather helped build). Gunter revealed that they played a lot in the Hitler Youth.

I looked on him as a friend and we got on well together. At Christmas I gave him a bundle of gifts including Christmas cake which he much appreciated. I've often wondered how he got on when they were repatriated back home but I never heard anything more.

From Jurby we used to walk a couple of miles down to Lhen Beach on the West Coast and muck about to pass the time. There were few houses but a good café where we could get egg, bacon and chips with a plateful of bread and real butter, and all that for three and sixpence.

One day we found a ballonet, a type of fishing float, on the beach. I tried my hand as a snake charmer! (Note the sharp crease in both the photo and my trousers!)

Then we formed a band and that's me on the left playing a whistle, Phil on the drum. The other pal may be Maurice

I moved into Air Traffic Control doing duty in the control tower and in the airfield caravan used for observing the runways. We were talking aircraft down or relaying a homing that someone with a DF loop would calculate. We would talk to the pilots, tell them to call when downwind, call when on finals, then grant permission to land.

An air view of Ramsey. Middle distance beyond the wharf is the accommodation for confined Italian and German civilians

One of the staff pilots used to fly every weekend over to Barrow-in-Furness in his Spitfire. One day when he was coming back the cloud was a bit low and he flew straight into Maughlod Head on the Isle of Man coast. That was the end of him, as if you fly at 250 miles an hour into a cliff face you don't tend to make it.

A brand new Seafire that crashed at Jurby.

The RN pilot failed to use flaps so he ran out of runway, had to brake hard which tipped the nose into the grass

72

One morning I had a pain in the side of my stomach and could feel a big bump which was sore. I went to the Doc who said it was a hernia. They flew me in an Anson from Jurby to Charmy Down, to be taken to RAF Cosford Hospital by lorry. I was in there for ten days to have my operation and recuperate.

Whilst I was in hospital there was a dental nurse who would visit all the patients for check-ups. She was the most beautiful nurse with gorgeous ginger-auburn hair, like a film star. She demonstrated how I should clean my teeth properly with the brush. I could have easily fallen in love with her, and I know she took a fancy to me too, but I was discharged and flown back to Jurby before I could continue the chase.

It was at this time that I first lost my temper with a superior (but not the last!) On Station Routine Orders a notice appeared which said that anyone who had been training as a pilot then made redundant could now apply to carry on their course by putting in their application to the CO.

I filled in the application form and handed it to the CO's adjutant, Flying Officer Reynolds. Reynolds was a F/O in rank only, as I had already heard on the grapevine that he was scrubbed from his pilot course in Canada after he landed an Oxford at night with the wheels up.

He took the form from me, and said, "What chance to do you think you've got? I've been trying to get back on the course and I can't do it!"

And he promptly rolled my form into a ball and threw it in the waste paper basket. I could understand him being bitter about his own failure but that was hardly my fault! I was red faced with anger, starting to resemble a ripe tomato, as I protested,

"You can't do that, Sir! The CO can do it, but you have no right to!"

I went away and wrote out another form, gave that to him, and made damn sure he took it in. As I had been talking back to him he could have put me forward for a reprimand, but he didn't do so as I am sure he knew he was very much in the wrong.

I met Reynolds again some years later after I had got my Wings. There was an important GCI (Ground Controlled Interception) Station at RAF Trimley Heath, near Felixstowe. When my fighter squadron came over from Germany for an exercise at RAF Wattisham we were taken there for a look round. As we walked in the door, the first person I saw was F/O Reynolds. He looked up at me, and as I looked back at him I tapped the wings on my chest, and nodded as if to say, "Yes mate, they are there. *I* made it!"

Anyway, the CO had my pilot application and he sent me over to the mainland a few weeks later for the first of two interviews to start the process.

From Jurby I went to another Air Crew Holding Unit, ACHU South Cerney near Cirencester, which was a nice place.

RAF South Cerney 1947

Top left is Ken Rooker, MUG, who ended up in my crew. Next is a Scotsman who owes me £2.50. I didn't drink or smoke so always had some money whilst the boozy chaps were always short. I lent him some cash and he got posted away and I rather think he knew he was going. Then it's me and I have no idea what I was holding up for the photo or why. Then Dunne.

Bottom left is a Scottish chap I got on well with who died with PII Wadley (see next chapter) and then two chaps with lots of Operational experience.

Chapter 12
Struck by the weather

I n July 1947 I was posted to RAF Lindholme, Yorkshire, to join 230 OCU (Operational Conversion Unit) where we learned to operate Lancaster bombers. I was crewed up with Wing Commander Frank Smith, DFC, who had been shot down in a Wellington early in the war and became a POW. He was a jolly good pilot and also a very decent chap. He was also converting to the Lanc and I was allocated as his rear gunner with Ken Rooker as mid upper gunner. I already knew Ken from Holding Unit and we got on very well. He would say "I'm a Yorkshire man, born and bred, strong in arm but weak in head." The only other crew name I remember is our navigator, Johnny Elvidge. The others have slipped my memory.

In the doorway of a Mk 1 (Far East) Lancaster with Ken Rooker at Lindholme

My great interest in the weather began when we were training on the Lancasters with Wingco Smith. We took off one evening from Lindholme and we flew straight up to 30,000 feet on our way to Brest on the west coast of France. As we went up the sun was setting, and the Alto Cumulus and Cirrus Cumulus clouds in the sky were showing in all different colours - green, gold and purple. Wow! I had never realised clouds could be so beautiful. When I got back to base I started finding out about clouds and environmental lapse rates, being the change of temperature with altitude, dependant on whether the air was saturated or not and other factors.

From that study I moved on to general weather interest and later became something of a weather expert, as I realised how important it was for a pilot to understand it well.

Somewhere over Portsmouth on our trip to Brest we were at 30,000 feet and the skipper said "Look, those are star shells there." And indeed, they were Royal Navy shells exploding at our height a few miles right in front of us.

Johnny the navigator said, "Shall we divert, skipper?"

"No, no, we will press on."

I was in the back listening to this exchange, thinking "Bloody hell, I hope my parachute is a good one."

Wingco Smith had been flying manually, holding the stick himself, towards Brest but after he turned us to head towards Paris he said, "I will go over to George now." (That's the automatic pilot.) I heard him say that and the next thing I knew my tail end went fifty feet up in the air, as down we sank, and my stomach was still up there somewhere on the roof of my turret. We plummeted 3,000 feet whilst he switched off George and regained control. He climbed us up again and said he would give it another try. He switched to George and this time I was ready when the same thing happened: up went the tail and down went the nose as we plummeted 3,000 feet in no time.

This proved to us that you need at least 3,000 feet to recover from a steep dive in a Lancaster. There were some valves in George and if one happened to get stuck it didn't work and properly caught you out. My stomach was grateful when the skipper said he would not try it for a third time! He would have been tired, as it was an eight hour trip in all, but he had to carry on flying by hand.

We headed back through quite a storm to Lindholme where we landed and went to the Mess at about 2:30 am for bacon and eggs to warm up. I had had icicles hanging from my mask it was so cold in the open rear turret. My electrical suit was playing up and not working for my left foot or my right glove so those were almost freezing.

As we sat there, someone said, "Why is Wadley not back yet? He was behind us somewhere."

PII Wadley was a nice bloke. I knew two of the crew and his rear gunner was a Scotsman I was very friendly with. We went to see Doncaster Rovers play Hull at football, where Jock was rooting for Hull as we stood amongst a crowd of Yorkshire miners who supported Doncaster. We got some menacing looks, and I said, "Jock, for God's sake, look around you!" He said "Och, forget that!" and the tough little man carried on regardless.

When having our mug of tea that very early morning someone came in and informed us that a police sergeant at the seafront in Skegness has reported seeing an aeroplane over The Wash that had suddenly exploded and crashed into the sea. We could only assume the aircraft was struck by lightning, and that it was not properly bonded. Every metal part has to be joined together, either riveted or joined with copper wire. If not, the gap between two pieces of metal can act like a spark plug, and anything like petrol fumes nearby could cause it to explode. A sad loss of those fine men that night.

In my flying suit at Lindholme

Chapter 13
Rear Gunner in 61 Squadron

Our crew was then posted to RAF Waddington where my memory is hazy. I believe Smith was to become the new CO (Flying) of 61 Squadron. We flew there in our Lancaster Mk 1 (Far East specification). We were due to convert to Avro Lincolns which had two 0.5 inch Browning cannons in the rear turret whilst the mid-upper gunner had two 20mm cannons to play with.

Ken in front of the rear turret of a new Lincoln that we were going to be flying

There is nothing much in my log book so we obviously didn't do much flying but we were at Waddington a few months and also a couple of months at RAF Hemswell.

It was from there we wanted to go into Lincoln one evening. Hemswell was only a couple of miles from the A15, an old Roman road known as Ermine Street, that ran straight down south towards Lincoln (until the runway extension for V-bombers at RAF Scampton caused a diversionary kink in the road, some years later.)

So we hopped on the bus thinking this trip won't take very long, and how wrong we were. There are two lines of villages that, like Hemswell, fall a few miles either side of the main road. Our bus zig-zagged across the A15 numerous times to visit each village, so by the time we finally arrived in Lincoln we had lost half the bloody evening! The next time we took a taxi.

Sometime during that period I was invited to RAF Cosford to have an interview regarding my pilot application.

Our crew at Lindholme or on 61 Squadron - left-right
W/Op Walker (?), Flight Engineer,
Pilot Wing Commander Frank George Laughton Smith, DFC,
MUG Ken Rooker, Navigator Johnny Elvidge, and the Bomb aimer.
I was the rear gunner and took the photograph

After some leave I got back to Waddington on a Monday morning when Wingco Smith asked me "Have you had your injections for the Middle East?" I said I hadn't. "Well go and get them, then. We are off to Egypt next week."

We were supposed to go off to Shallufa Airfield (near the Suez Canal) on the coming Sunday so I was booked in on Wednesday morning at Nocton Hall, the RAF hospital a couple of miles from Waddington. When I arrived for the jabs the MO said "You want all of them? Today?" I said that was the plan and was given yellow fever, typhoid and cholera jabs in my arm, one after the other. They were supposed to allow a fortnight between each injection, but there wasn't time for that. By that same evening I was in hospital. I was laid up in bed feeling weak and bloody awful, but I said to the nurse the next morning, "Look I have to get out of here and get cleared, as I have to go to overseas on Sunday."

She said, "You don't go anywhere until the MO says so." I asked where he was, to which she replied, "I don't know at the moment, but until he comes and sees you, you stay put."

On Friday the same thing happened, no sign of the MO. On Saturday I said to the nurse, "I am in real trouble now, I have to have everything ready in my turret, and my kit ready to go off tomorrow morning, and I am still not cleared."

She said, "You stay there, Sergeant, until the MO comes!" And I never did see the bloody MO.

But on that Saturday morning a Corporal came in with a telegram for me. I was still feeling very weak so I said, "You open it," thinking if it was a telegram, it must be bad news. He thought the same, as he said "No, no, I can't open it, it might be bad news." So I did, and read:

"GO HOME MONDAY 10 DAYS LEAVE "

... and I was thinking "Oh no, I've just been on leave, so something has happened at home!" but it went on ...

"REPORT RAF SHELLINGFORD FOR INITIAL PILOT TRAINING"

Hurrah!

I did as I was told. I never went to Egypt and never found out how my crew got on without me. I was surprised that Wing Commander Smith or one of the others didn't at least come to see me in hospital to see how I was. What I didn't know until much later was that Smith had recommended me for a commission, which was on my RAF Form 1369. As a Wing Commander (Flying) he was entitled to have all his crew commissioned, but because I moved on to the pilot's course I missed out. At that time commissions weren't being awarded to my intake of pilots under training, so I missed out again. Be warned that I shall continue to bemoan that fact!

Our navigator wanted to get married so he borrowed £5 off all the crew, but then I got posted on my pilot's course and never got the money back. There was another chap who I lent two and a half quid to, as well as the chap at South Cerney, so overall I was down ten quid in unrepaid loans during my RAF days!

How did I spend my leave periods now I was back in England after the Isle of Man? I went back to see Mam, Sep, Ella and little John in Felling. I still had my bicycle at this time and at a dance found a lovely girlfriend, Betty Duff, who was a bit older than me in her early twenties.

She lived at Wallsend where she worked for a commercial laundry, checking items in and out with laundry marks. Betty lived on the opposite shore to Felling where the Roman wall ends. It was only about two miles as the crow flies, but I had to cycle three miles along to the main Tyne bridge, over that and then three miles back to her place. We would just walk around the town and along the river together and go dancing at the Oxford Galleries.

Betty had a very vivacious sister and the two of them could converse with all their words backwards and quite quickly too. It was most impressive and I was unable to catch more than the odd word when they were at it! Ragus (sugar) was one I remember picking out.

One day my mother said to me, "I like Betty." Unknown to me, Betty had been to visit her when I was away. Betty was too nice for me as I didn't want to settle at that stage, and knew I would be moving around a lot, so we parted ways.

At a dance back home I met another Tyneside girl called Cynthia and we went out for a year or so. She was very worldly wise and seemed to like her oats, anywhere and anytime it seemed, and I was happy to give her some of mine.

One of our first coastal liaisons was on a bus trip day outing with her firm to Bamburgh Castle near Lindisfarne. We walked on the beach and found a cosy little nest in the sand dunes. She was great as she knew all the tricks and became my first lover.

Cynthia's sister was an accountant on the west coast near Millfield so we went to stay for the weekend when I was on leave. We went over there on a crowded bus, and although I managed to get Cynthia a seat I had to stand all the way, for sixty miles, hanging on to a strap. We stayed with her sister and had to sleep in separate rooms, but we had a walk along the beach at night which made for an amorous weekend.

Before I went to Germany we had a weekend together at The Blue Ram Hotel in Grantham and then another weekend in a York guest house. She put on an old ring she had found - probably a brass curtain ring - to pretend we were married. But there were two old men in the lobby who guessed we were not married and it was all a ruse. They were grinning as they kept loudly asking me questions like, "So how much is the marriage allowance you get in the Air Force?" They simply wouldn't give up and I got more and more embarrassed!

Then at some point I finished with Cynthia as I jolly well knew she wasn't the type of girl who would wait for me when I was sent overseas. I knew she would just go dancing and meet somebody else.

On one trip home I met two of my old teachers on the tram car going to Newcastle. I got on at Felling, went upstairs, and there they were sitting together in uniform. Mr. Wilson was a Corporal in the Army and Mr. Nelson was a Sergeant Navigator. I was on leave from Cannock and had my white flash on my hat, signifying aircrew. They must have noticed me but showed no interest and I didn't dare speak to them.

Lincoln Cathedral was what the boys looked for when coming back from raids. When they spotted the spires they knew they were nearly home

Chapter 14

A couple of prangs at Pilot School...

but my Wings, at last!

W e had some basic flying instruction in 3 EFTS, the Elementary Flying Training School, at RAF Shellingford in Berkshire (now part of Oxfordshire).

They wanted to see if we could fly solo within 12 hours training which would qualify us to begin proper pilot training. My instructor was a quietly spoken chap called PII Godfree with whom I got on well. I was progressing nicely with my instruction when disaster struck! Godfree went off on leave and I was handed over to PII Ernie Tune with whom my time in the air was one long shouting tirade: Look at your wings! Look at your airspeed! What are you doing with your nose position! and so on *ad nauseum* until I started to feel useless and that I couldn't do anything right for him.

Then followed a stroke of luck. Fog came and enveloped our small, grassy airfield which stopped all flying for a few days. As the fog cleared one morning, in walked Mr. Godfree and all was well! I began to enjoy flying again in a civilised manner with a fine instructor.

I had two final tests with officer instructors F/O Thompson and F/O Brown. The second of these tests was a worry as, when I came back into the airfield circuit, I could see I hadn't lost enough height and was much too high to begin my descent. I suddenly felt a panic! Everything had gone so well (apart from Tune's tuition) and now I had made a problem. Brown asked me, "What are you going to do?"

I replied, "I'll have to go round again, Sir."

"I'm glad you decided that. Go ahead," so around I went and this time made a lovely, gentle, floating descent to touch down in an excellent landing.

They were happy, I had passed, and I was sent up alone! I soloed for ten minutes on 22nd of January 1948, after 8 hours and 45 minutes of flying, and Godfree was very chuffed. As for me, I was up somewhere at 90,000 feet floating with joy!

I don't know what became of those who failed, poor devils; it must have been an awful feeling not seeing your name on the Pass List.

A quick side note on the ranks. For a few years after the war the RAF brought in a new P system for Non-Commissioned Officers.

- PIV ("Pee Four"), one star, for Leading Aircraftman. That was us.
- PIII, two stars
- PII, three stars, Sergeant
- PI, three stars and crown, Flight Sergeant.

When I was PIV - with one star, not the four you might expect! - a couple of us went to a dance and were chatting to some girls. One of them asked me, "What is that star on your sleeve for?"

"Oh, we are senior officers, the top brass! One Star is like a General, I suppose."

"Ooh," she cooed. And we got a dance.

It must have been a very boozy afternoon when they came up with that silly P system which confused everyone. I became PIII later, after I got my Pilot's Wings, and after I was posted to Germany they dropped the system and I became a Sergeant Pilot with three stripes. All became clear again!

Gunner IV at Isle of Man

Next it was ITS (Initial Training School) at RAF Wittering where we did drill, physical training, navigation, airmanship, and learned about engines. The teacher talked about pistons, con-rods, carburettors and so on. Most of the other cadets were flight engineers so our teacher was preaching to the converted with them, leaving only me who was clueless in that department. We were there for 20 weeks and it wasn't until week 19 that, for me, petrol engines really fell into place and I "got" how they worked. (We only began to look at jet engines later, when I went to jet school.)

I was very pleased to be reunited with my chum Ronnie "Jock" Queen and we often played one another at table tennis. One evening after tea we played for so long we forgot to go off to the night briefing. After we rolled up late we got the job of cleaning the crew room for the next fortnight.

Self and Ronnie Queen under training in Tiger Moths

The U/T Pilots at ITS Wittering No. 12 Pilot Course, July 1948

Rear row:
1. John Hugh McDaid 2. Sid Hyams 3. Pete T. Cunnington
4. Self 5. Johnnie E. C. Briers

   Middle Row:
1. A. A. "Lofty" Holyoake 2. A.S "Stan" Foulkes 3. Ronnie "Jock" Queen
4. Ronnie J. Guy 5. F. A. Brown 6. Bernard Bolton
7. R. G. "Clewey" Coleman

Bottom Row:
1. F. S. J. Sid Aldridge 2. S. T. G. "Gwyn" Price 3. Flt Lt V. George Gibbard
4. L. R. "Taffy" Needes 5. Peter W. Grant

I will tell a bit about the sixteen U/T Pilot boys on my course, and our instructor, as far as I can recall the details.

Hugh McDaid was an ex-AG who made it through the course. I never saw him again, except one day a few years later I was going on the bus up the A1 to Tyneside. I was looking out of the window near Burghley horse showground where I saw a chap lying down having a nap. Just then, he happened to sit up and it was McDaid! I heard he had been friendly with a barmaid in Stamford and put her in the family way.

Sid Hyams made it through but I never saw him again.

Pete Cunnington was my room mate. He was always popping off to London to see his girlfriend, possibly in the plural as he was a real Casanova. One day he said to me, "Have you ever seen crabs?"

"Oh yes, I've seen a crab at the beach."

"No, no, I mean crabs on the body. Look at these!"

He showed me them in his pubic area and I was quite shocked! I expect he had been with a girl that he would have best avoided.

Briers killed himself on Mosquitos, I heard somewhere. It had a peculiar twist to it, torque under take off, and you had to be ready for that and hold against it. That could have done for him, perhaps.

Lofty Holyoake was a good lad who had been a corporal in the clothing stores and who made it out as a pilot.

Stan Foulkes had been a flight engineer and he made it, but we didn't get on as I found him a bit of a stuffy know-all.

Jock Queen was my pal, a great friend, so more about him later.

Ron Guy was a good friend who came from Reading. He had been a flight engineer on Halifaxes flying out of Tiree on the west coast of Scotland on meteorological flights consisting of three legs across the ocean. First leg outward at 18,000 feet, for the second leg spiral down to 500 or 1,000 feet then climb back up to 18,000 feet for the home leg. He said he found "Tiree as boring as hell" and they ate eggs for most meals until they were sick of the sight them. Sadly, he had to drop out as he and his wife would lose their marriage allowance if he became a cadet pilot.

Brown had been a medical student and was a bit of a nutter in my opinion. I remember him swinging a kitten in a bucket, round and round, to see if it would black out. Of course, it didn't. We blacked out because if we turned tightly, the blood drained away from the heart and the brain, but the kitten was horizontal in the bucket so that didn't happen and it was just cruel.

I didn't ever go in a g-force machine, but they made us go without oxygen until we blacked out and would recognise the sensation. If you see two grey rings coming, ease off - let the stick go. I rather think Brown died on Mosquitoes too.

Bernard Boulton, I heard on the grapevine, killed himself on Mosquitoes soon after he joined a Squadron.

Clewey (Clueless) Coleman was a nice lad and more about him later and a mid-air collision!

Sid Aldridge went off to fly bombers. We had all been on Lancs and most chaps wanted to fly them, but I preferred the idea of fighters, and in particular the Typhoons that I had so admired from Acklington.

Gwyn Price was our course Flight Leader who went on Lancs and ended up as a Sqn Ldr with DFM. I was in email contact with him up to about ten years ago.

Flt Lt George Gibbard was an ex-bomber pilot with Post Traumatic Stress Disorder which meant he couldn't fly anymore, so he became a ground instructor and was a lovely bloke. PTSD is not the same as LMF (lack of moral fibre) at all. One day on parade George started wandering around talking to himself whilst everyone else was at ramrod attention. One of the other instructors went over to say, "Come on, George", and then took his hand to lead him away.

Taffy Needes was another flight engineer who had a wife and children and had to withdraw. A great pity to lose those chaps for that reason. At one Air Crew Association meeting I showed this group picture and it was lovely when a chap called out, "That's Taffy Needes!"

Pete Grant I don't remember much about.

Some of the above is hearsay which means I can't be sure of my facts and I do occasionally get names a bit muddled these days. I apologise if there are any errors. If anyone knows any different stories or further information about these old flying chums, I would love to hear it.

Some of the chaps sitting on a car at RAF Wittering, for no particular reason!

Back:
Self,
Sid Aldridge,
Ron Queen,
Ron Guy,
Hugh Mcdaid

Middle:
Taffy Needes,
Clewey Coleman,
Johnny Briers

Bottom: Pete Cunnington

Myself and Ronnie Guy, previously a flight engineer, who had a camera.

After No 12 Pilot Course we were posted to RAF Cottesmore 7 FTS (Flight Training School) in Rutland. When I arrived, the very first pilot instructor I saw was PII Ernie Tune! My heart sank, thinking that if I get him as my full-time instructor I will have no chance of making the grade. Thank goodness I didn't get lumbered with him! I got PII George Watts, another lovely man and fine instructor who was as good for me as PII Godfree had been. Watts had been an operational pilot but he never told me what he flew or where.

Pete Cunnington, my room mate, with a Tiger Moth

All was going well on de Havilland DH 82a Tiger Moth biplanes with Watts as my instructor until 27th August 1948, the day before my 22nd birthday.

It was a lovely August evening. After tea all thirteen remaining pupils and their instructors went back to the grass area to do some dual circuits and landings followed by a solo of the same.

The drill we were given was to take off, climb at 70 knots to 1,000 feet, turn downwind for 1,000 feet, turn round on finals, and land. The dual trip went without drama and then I was lined up for take-

91

off to do what would be my second solo flight at 7 FTS, and third solo in all.

All the instructors were sitting to watch each of their pupils. I taxied to the take off point, opened up the throttle and took off, climbing at 70 knots as instructed. I got to 400ft, happy as Larry, when suddenly there was a big bang. I was jolted up and I found myself standing on my starboard wing tip, wondering, "What the hell is going on?" Out of the corner of my eye I was aware of something fluttering down to the ground.

All I could think was, "Am I flying? Yes, I am still flying!" I righted the Moth and gingerly climbed to the circuit height of 1,000 feet. I realised that someone must have collided with me but I found the aircraft was flying quite normally so could only wonder where I had been hit. I stuck to the plan and came downwind at a thousand feet, still shaking like a leaf, and then I spotted a crashed biplane burning on the ground. I thought, "You poor sod," assuming he was dead. It also flashed through my mind that it might be my best pal Jock.

As I turned back on to base leg and into my final approach I decided to carry out a precautionary landing at only 40 knots or so, "hanging on the prop" as they say, in deference to some likely damage below. I touched down and immediately spun round to port and came to a very abrupt halt. I climbed out and the Safety Officer, Flt Lt Holmes came rushing over from his Jeep to ask if I was all right.

I replied, "Yes Sir, I am fine. Who was in the crashed kite?"

"Coleman, but he got out okay."

"Really? Out of that?" I couldn't believe it!

Coleman was called Clewey, short for Clueless, and he didn't seem to mind his nickname. He had been the next up after me and hadn't followed the instructions. Instead of climbing as intended he had held his nose down too long so that when he did come up he was underneath me. His right wingtip had crippled my left wheel strut, which is why my wheel collapsed on landing, and the damage to his wing had put him in a spin from which he had no chance to recover from that height.

Holmes said I had done a good job landing my damaged plane safely, and that I would get a green endorsement in my logbook. However, in the Court of Inquiry they said, "Both pilots should have

92

kept a better lookout". I have always smarted at that comment because I could not possibly see Clewey coming up behind and below me! That decision meant I did not get the endorsement, which was the first of two times it was suggested that I be endorsed but it was never actioned.

Clewey got out of that burning aeroplane so quick that he undid every strap, including his wristwatch it seems, as his Omega service watch was never found. I was astounded to find that he had jumped out without a scratch from a spin into the ground from 400 feet.

Clewey's second-hand kite for sale, all offers considered

Clewey got through his training on Tiger Moths but when we got onto Harvards, where we had to be able to recover from a spin on instruments to get our White Card, he couldn't do it. I suppose it was something in his head after that fiery episode. I was sorry he got dismissed to civvy street as everybody liked him.

A couple of months later my instructor, PII Watts, and I went off with a full load of fuel around the low flying area, where I did some aerobatics and practised forced landings. We came back and landed, and he got out and said, "Right off you go, exactly

My kite repaired with a new strut but the dent is still visible in the main spar

the same exercise solo, for another hour and a quarter."

We had to do 70 hours on Tiger Moths before going on to Harvards. I wanted every possible minute in my log book to make up those hours, so off I went to enjoy myself for almost the allotted time before I returned to land. As I was coming round on finals, out of nowhere came another Tiger Moth, straight in from the low flying area, which was the wrong thing to do and he cut me off. I had to climb away and go round again at 400 feet but my engine cut out. Oh bugger! My fuel gauge was still showing fuel, a quarter of an inch above empty.

I shoved the stick forward and the engine picked up again. I turned round and came downwind when the engine cut out again, and I had no option but to force land right where I was. Ahead of me was a triangular field of cattle and I quickly decided I could side-slip in there and hopefully not run into the hedge on the far boundary. I hit the deck about a third of the way into the field and shot across it. Fortunately, the cows scattered as I came in or it would have been a bloody mess, even without the propeller under power.

My wings hit the electric fence, pushed it over, and I went just into the hedge until the resilience of the fence and hedge branches pushed me back out again. The plane was not badly damaged at all, it just had the tail skid broken off as it sprang out backwards, and the wings were scuffed where they brought the fence posts back more or less upright again.

Flt Lt Holmes had been alerted and when he arrived he looked around and, because the fence post was there behind my wing, he said, "Oh, so you dropped down like that into the hedge?" Silly bugger! No one could come down like that in one piece.

"No, Sir, I rolled in and out again. As you can see there is yellow paint on both sides of the post."

He said, "Really? Well done! You'll get a green endorsement for this forced landing," but just like before, I never did.

There was a Court of Inquiry and my instructor got a reprimand for putting me up for so long. Two and half hours was on the limit of safe endurance of the Tiger Moth fuel system, especially whilst doing exercises that required a lot of full throttle work. That decision was unfair on both of us. If I had not been cut off by the other pilot (and we never found out who that bugger was) all would have been fine, if a bit tight, and if the fuel gauge had been reliable I would have come in sooner anyway.

We moved onto flying monoplane Harvards where among the many things we learned was bombing with 25 pounders clipped under the wing. You would fly to the target, get the target positioned in front of the port wing, and as it comes out behind the wing, you roll over into a dive and let one go. I achieved some very near misses and it was certainly great fun.

The Harvard trainer, a great plane, flown by one of my mates

By the time you are flying a Harvard, which is a lovely and powerful aeroplane, you are pretty proficient. There was a Czech pilot PI Fras who wanted to go to RAF Ouston, presumably to see a girl. He knew I came from near there and he asked me, "Would you fly me up to Ouston? We will have the weekend off, then you fly me back on the Monday?" I said, "Yes, of course I will!" Off we went and marked it down as a navigation training flight for me.

When we arrived I got some grub in the mess and spotted Joyce, my lovely, pretty friend from Dolcis Shoes! I was delighted to see her

95

again and learned she had joined the WAAF not long after I had left. I don't know how she managed to do that as an unmarried mother, probably her own mother looked after the kid, but I don't know. She said another girl we knew from the shop had joined the Army so perhaps I had started an exodus!

I left the airfield to visit my family and my girlfriend in Felling and the only problem was getting a lift back to Ouston, ten miles west of Newcastle, early on the Monday morning.

Keep Fit at Cottesmore - myself nearest and clearly the finest specimen!

About a week before getting our Wings we had a final Instrument Flying test with the IF testing officer. We had an amber screen and blue goggles, so that you can't see outside, and the goggles had a little tube that was set outside the canopy so that you got fresh air to prevent the goggles from steaming up. Unfortunately my pipe had been squashed by the hood of the Harvard which meant that one eyepiece misted up and I could only see with the other. Not surprisingly I made a right old balls-up of the exercise. The instructor had no patience and told me I was useless. I told him I was steamed up, but he didn't care and wouldn't let me go up again. Instead I had to rearrange a second test with him, worryingly close to the end of the course, where I made very sure my pipes were intact! All went swimmingly well that second time.

So... I had passed the course! There were 16 U/T (under training) pilots on my Cottesmore course. Three of them didn't make it as they were married, and as they didn't get the full pay allowance U/T, they found their wives couldn't manage financially and they had to drop out. Two of the others didn't make it through the course for various reasons, leaving eleven of us who gained our Wings.

We had our Wings Presentation Parade at the airfield on 10th August 1948, and then in the evening we had a party at the Ram Jam Inn just up the road on the A1. We were all smart in polished shoes and our best uniform with our Wings newly sewn on. I went there on the back of a motorbike with a chap called Phil. We had a great evening and both of us were a bit sozzled when we came out to head back to camp. It wasn't far to go but it was a twisty road. Suddenly we found we were scooting across the road to hit a wall and bounced back, skidding along on our bottoms. The problem was that the tyre had burst but we didn't realise that until we remounted and tried again, rolled along for a short way and promptly fell off again. I had scuffed up my best uniform with holes in my pants and elbows and my new shoes had wedges ground off the heels!

Back: Jock Brown, Syd Hyams, Me, Lofty Holyoake,
Bernard Bolton, John Hugh McDaid
Front: Ronnie Queen, Johnnie Briers, Gwyn Price,
Pete Grant, Sid Aldridge

After finishing at Cottesmore I moved on to join air traffic control with 240 OCU at RAF North Luffenham for three months. This was just another "ghost posting" (filling in time, waiting for the next proper posting) and nothing much happened.

98

Chapter 15
Jet School at Driffield

RAF Driffield, east of York towards Bridlington on the Yorkshire coast, was the home of the brand new jet school equipped with twin engine Gloster Meteors and single engine de Havilland Vampires.

I started off in the Meteor Mk 7 two seater with my instructor, PII Jock Riddoch. We did 4½ hours together before I did half an hour solo in it.

As soon as I came down from that, he said "Ok, now you are going off in the Vampire." That was very much a single-seater so you simply had to go it alone.

He took me across to it, I climbed in and my first thought was, "Where's the aeroplane?" All you've got is a little nose and the wings are back behind you somewhere, quite different to the Meteor. My second thought was, "Blimey, it's a bit cramped in this tiny cockpit!"

I had already read the flying manual and we went over the controls. Riddoch then gave me the drill. "Go up to 6,000 feet, do some clean stalls and then try some dirty stalls, then you can have fun with some aerobatics."

So up I went, and at 6,000 feet I did clean stalls - flaps in, wheels in, dive brakes in - that was a piece of cake and good fun.

I climbed back up to 6,000 and started the dirty stall routine - flaps out, wheels down, dive brakes out - and whoosh, I was straight into a spin. I was spinning down to the right, so I thought, "OK, stick forward, opposite rudder" and that stopped it all right - but now I was spinning to the left! Same thing again, I tried to correct that and went spinning back the other way.

I could see the trees coming up on the west side of Bridlington. Christ! How am I going to stop this! My heart was right up in my throat. I decided to try half-rudder, and the Vamp came out of the spin and into my control with a series of flicks.

I had gone off as brave as a lion but came home like a jelly. I had been looking forward to doing the aerobatics but didn't even bother as I was so bloody frightened. When those trees were only about 500 feet away and I realised one and a half more turns and I would be plunged into the deck...

I got back to the base and told Jock about my ordeal.

"Vampires don't spin," he said.

"They bloody well do! Mine certainly did!"

Some of the pilots on Course 3, Driffield. 1949
Back (NCOs): Self, Peter Clayton and Ronnie Queen, good mates together.
Front (Officers): Ollie Burton and Flt Lt Phipps (a bit pompous, always wore his peaked cap) and I can't remember the others.

A Driffield Vampire (photo from George Aird with thanks)

I was on Course Number 3, and I saw a lad who was coming towards the end of Course Number 2 kill himself one morning. He was PII Rees, a Welshman, who I never met in person.

I was up in the crew room where we saw a Meteor taxiing out, take off and fly north towards the Yorkshire Moors. As we were watching we heard a roar and could see a red glow. "Christ! he's flown into the bloody hills!" It was terrible to watch.

The Court of Inquiry was held at Driffield; one of my mates who had also been watching with me was called on to give evidence but we knew little that could help them. They think they know why it happened. In the aircraft you have the artificial horizon instrument which you live by as it stays constant so that you can always see your angle. The instrument has a metal body with four little doors, but on acceleration it can get a bit out of synchronisation and give a slightly false reading, making it look as if you are climbing more steeply than you are. They decided that his artificial horizon reading might have confused him, so he levelled off and clipped the hills. He was more experienced than me so he shouldn't have made that mistake, if that really was the explanation.

Tall and strong, I was one of his pall bearers. On the day of his departure from the RAF Station we loaded his coffin onto a lorry and took him to the railway station, where we offloaded his casket into a goods wagon that stunk of fish. I thought how bloody awful that the poor boy has to go home in a stinking fish wagon.

Socalising - Ronnie Queen, Jock Riddoch, self and Danny Schnitzler, a Czech.

A Meteor at Driffield

One weekend I went to a dance and met a nurse. I walked her back and we had a good old snog. I invited her out for a drink the next day and she suggested a pub along the Bridlington sea front. I met her there the next night where we had a drink together followed by a walk along the beach. I laid my greatcoat down so we could sit on it and we got a bit amorous. All these coastal encounters with girls: it must have been something in the sea air! I never saw her again.

After I passed my Jet School course at Driffield I was posted to 226 OCU at RAF Stradishall in Suffolk. The Operational Conversion Unit was where, having learned to fly a jet fighter, I had to learn how to use it effectively in combat. I did three months there on how to really use the Vampire. Gunnery, rockets, aerobatics, formation flying, the lot. The rockets were always fakes, as the MOD didn't have the spare cash for us to "waste" real ones. The key thing was to learn the angle and speeds of attack. You followed the instructor who would show the required angles of dive.

Half of the Vampire Cockpit

I took off one morning and headed into Norfolk, right round the coast on a low-level trip. At Wells-next-the-Sea there were some Army ack-ack gunners doing firing practice, and they were still firing while a string of us were flying through. I reported back over the R/T that we were being fired upon at the Norfolk coast!

102

I was starting my turn to head back round the coast at Cromer when I got a call: "Return to base immediately. Fog imminent." I opened up the throttle and set off like a madman. When I got to the railway line between Ipswich, Bury and Cambridge, I could see a thick fog had already taken hold of the area.

I thought, "Oh bugger!" Like a fool I dropped down into the fog to see if I could see the deck. After a minute or two I suddenly remembered the highest point in Suffolk is 420 feet, at Chedburgh, only a few miles from Stradishall. I pulled up out of the fog and asked for a diversion instead. They diverted me to RAF Lakenheath which was an American MATS transport base.

I called for landing instructions and they talked me in. I taxied in, went to the tower and told them I was from Stradishall up the road, which was fog bound.

They said, "You are welcome here, and safe for now."

"Can your guys kindly service my plane and refuel it?" I had used most of my fuel with the low-flying and the high-speed dash.

"No, sorry pal, we don't have any jet aviation fuel here, only 100 octane petrol." That was the stuff they used in their big transport planes.

So I was stuck there for a night and two days. Of course, I had no overnight gear with me, just my flying suit, gloves and helmet. I was allocated to a Sergeant in the Sergeants' Mess. He introduced me to the One-Armed Bandits, where you put your dollars and dimes in and lose it all. They simply called them The Robbers, but they still played them!

Stradishall eventually sent a bowser to Lakenheath to refuel me. I did my own DI, as we were taught how to do our Daily Inspection in case of a diversion such as this. I was ready to go, when the tower asked, "Would you give us a low flypast when you go?" Wow! Being asked to do that? Of course I would! I went out, turned around, and went roaring past at 450 knots over their base. "Thank you, Sir, and have a nice day!" they said. What splendid chaps!

Next, I had another time-killing posting to RAF Hednesford up in Staffordshire for a month or two whilst waiting to be posted to a squadron. That was an experience. They were taking in old junk from all the airfields to dispose of, like we had done at Stafford. I was given charge of twenty Italian POWs who were moving things about using Lister trucks, which were little wagons with an engine on a platform. I had to pick these guys up from their camp at 08:30 in the morning, and by about 08:45 I couldn't find any of them! They were crafty buggers. They knew I was only a rookie, not knowing the ropes, and they did just what they liked.

They had their skiving very well organised. At one spot behind a hangar was a line of the huge wooden packing cases, used for engines and aircraft parts, and now standing empty. One day I happened to see a man sneaking through a hole in one of the cases, so I followed him inside and through two more cases until I found their den at the end. By the time I got there they had all scarpered through a bolthole. I discovered they had even rigged up wingtip lights, wired up with batteries, so they could signal to each other if anyone was coming! I decided I wouldn't waste my time trying to discipline these idlers. They were very crafty in doing as little work as possible, but when I did catch up with them for long enough I did manage to get some work out of them.

Finally, I heard what I was destined to do! A posting to West Germany in the height of the Cold War with the USSR.

We were sent down to RAF Northolt, Middlesex, in preparation for going out to Europe in March 1950. I was delighted to be going with my best pal Ronnie Queen and other chums.

We had a couple of days to wait there and someone suggested we went to the Windmill Theatre in the West End of London, which was renowned for their saucy nudes. Well, frankly, they weren't! On the side of the stage were near-naked ladies, who didn't move, wearing some kind of body stocking. Mind you, that did not stop a number of men in the front rows from ogling them all over with binoculars!

It was all very disappointing except the one highlight of the evening being Arthur English, in his great big kipper tie, who was cracking very funny jokes all the time.

The next day we took off from Northolt in a Dakota and landed in Buckeburg, which was the main transit station for arriving and departing Germany.

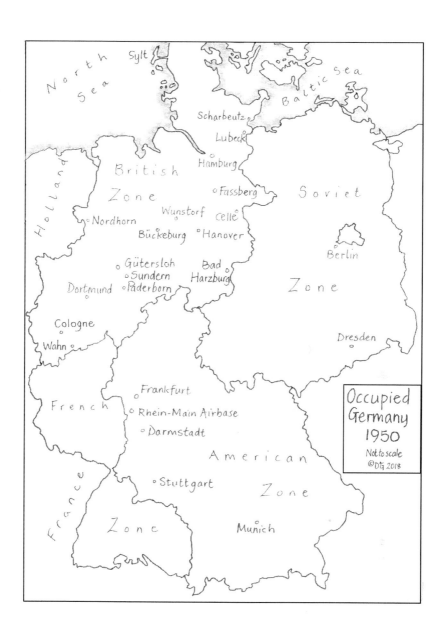

North Sea

Sylt

Baltic Sea

Scharbeutz

Lübeck

Hamburg

British Zone

Fassberg

Soviet

Wunstorf   Celle

Nordhorn

Holland

Bückeburg   Hanover

Berlin

Gütersloh   Bad

Sundern   Harzburg

Dortmund   Paderborn

Zone

Cologne

Wahn

Dresden

Frankfurt

French

Rhein-Main Airbase

Darmstadt

American

Stuttgart

Zone

France

Zone

Munich

Occupied
Germany
1950

Not to scale
©DG 2018

105

The following morning I was shaving when a Scotsman came in, at least half-drunk, and cut himself with his razor in a few places. I asked someone about him who said, "Ah yes. The Geek! He is wildly eccentric and always drunk: Some of these wartime blokes are very odd in their behaviour, you know, which is hardly surprising."

We were driven out to RAF Gütersloh where I was posted to 16 Squadron and most disappointed to be split from my pals, Jock Queen and Pete Clayton, who were put into 3 Squadron based at the same Station.

We were all very ready and willing for any action that may occur in Europe. I was never nervous and was ready for anything. I originally joined up prepared to die in the war, and it was still the same, only now I was equipped to defend Germany (or at least the West part) instead of attacking her.

It had taken me six years to achieve my dream of becoming a fighter pilot. Had I been born two years earlier I might have been in action with an older member of my ATC Squadron in Felling-on-Tyne, Colin Colquhoun, who not only saw war action but earned a DFC. He managed to do what I had dreamed of, having seen it on newsreels in the cinema. He was flying a Typhoon Mark I, a rocketeer's joy, blasting German tanks and lorries during the Falaise Gap massacre. The losses were high doing these vital but dangerous diving attacks, but he survived that and went on to fly Vampires after the war, like me.

Chapter 16
A Cold War posting to RAF Gütersloh

Finally, here I was - a fighter pilot on an active squadron in the 2nd Tactical Air Force.

Ronnie Queen in a 3 Squadron Vampire at Gütersloh

I had been there only a day or two when my new boss, Squadron Leader Lenny Lambert DFC, called for me. He said "Ralph, come in and sit down." Now that was a surprise, referring to a mere Sergeant Pilot by his first name.

He said "You are the first pilot we have had from that new jet school at Driffield. Tell me about it. What was the course like?"

I told him about it and answered the questions he put to me. I went on to tell him about my near-fatal spin when the instructor told me to try the dirty stall in the Vamp.

Boss Lambert said "Hang on a minute. Go back. It might be your accent, but it sounded to me like you said you went into a deliberate spin at only 6,000 feet! Tell me again what your instructor asked you to do?"

I repeated the instructions. Go to 6,000 feet, do clean stalls, then dirty stalls, then do some aerobatics.

He said, "Well then, you are bloody lucky to be alive."

"Sir?"

"I was on the Vampire team in 1946 at West Raynham when we did the spinning trials. We wouldn't start a deliberate spin under

25,000 feet. To start one at 6,000 feet is suicide. You are lucky to be here."

I replied, "To be honest, yes, I thought I'd had my chips when I saw the ground coming up."

He told me what it was like spinning from 25,000 feet. If they had not recovered by 10,000 feet they were instructed to bail out! He said, "The thing is, the Vampire has two little rudders, but they are very, very effective. That is the secret. Treat them with care."

It seems I probably had more rudder on than I realised when I did the dirty stall, and that's what started that fearful spin. I can still see those trees...

I have no idea whether Lambert passed that warning on to Jock Riddoch or not. Perhaps my instructor should have been told off, as that altitude was clearly far too low to try that trick. He might have got a reprimand if I had died, although only he and I knew that I had been told to dirty stall at just 6,000 feet.

I snapped this plane coming into Gütersloh not long after I arrived...
it turned out to be NATO chief General Eisenhower passing through.

In those days there was no single official RAF display team and most fighter squadrons had some sort of team of boys who wanted to do some tight formations and aerobatics. Lenny Lambert, or the AOC Earl Bandon, or both, had the crazy idea of a Vampire aerobatic team joined together with parachute elastic!

I had not long been there when the Boss said to me, "I want you to go to the clothing store at RAF Sylt and pick up all their parachute elastic and bring it back here." Parachute elastic is used to keep the covers on parachutes to keep them stowed. The Boss would have put out an enquiry to all stations to ask who had plenty available, and Sylt was the answer.

Off I went in my Vampire to Sylt, which is a T-shaped island on the west coast of Germany, joined to the mainland by a causeway just south of the Danish border. I got to know it well, later on, as that was where we went for a month twice a year, summer and winter, for weaponry practice on their firing ranges.

I was at 25,000 feet and could see Sylt, but to my alarm I could also see a layer of haar, very low-lying cloud, right down on the deck. (A cold sea fog, as most would probably call it.) This haar was moving in to the coast and I realised it was beating me to it, and that I might not get down before it enveloped the airfield lying in the centre of the island only a mile from the coast.

So... dive brakes out, full throttle, down like a rocket! I kept screaming down in a big wide sweeping circle, by which time I could already see the airfield gradually disappearing. To my great relief I spotted a Spitfire with its wheels down. "Great! A staff pilot," I thought, "he'll know where he is. I'll stick with him."

He was coming round at about 120 knots, as I was coming round doing 350. I throttled back and put the brakes out to get my speed down to under 200.

He descended into the bank of fog. I had to get lined up quick, so I stayed to his right and followed him into the fog. Suddenly he popped out of the cloud, dropped onto the runway, and so did I. Thank God! He went down the runway and I went belting past him doing nearly twice his speed. I had to brake like mad and when I finally parked it up and went in the Mess, I heard a very cross voice, asking, "Who the bloody hell was that in the Vampire?"

I went over and said, quietly, "Me. Thank you very much for being there. If you hadn't, I would have been in real trouble. I would've probably had to bail out over Denmark."

"Huh, Oh, mmm, I see," he grunted, as my sincere thanks had calmed him down quite a bit. I had given him one a hell of shock, of course, as I was on a different radio channel so he knew nothing about me being there as I shot past him on his runway.

I must say I really didn't want to bail out over Denmark, and then make my way back to base and have to tell my new Boss a) I hadn't made it b) I hadn't got his parachute elastic and c) I had lost his bloody aeroplane!

At that time no one had bailed out of a Vampire as far as I knew. It had no ejector seat. We did have one of our chaps bail out later, in thick cloud, but we don't know how he managed to get out. Jettisoning the hood was very easy; simply pull the lever and it would fly off and disappear and you were sitting on your parachute. But the Vampire was so cramped that it was difficult even on the ground to undo your straps, and if one of them didn't come free...

Much later I flew the Meteor Mark 8 that was equipped with an ejector seat. You ditch the canopy, reach up and pull down the handle of the blind that covers and protects your face and off you go! I never got to try it, I am glad to say.

Anyway, back to business! I went along to the stores and said to the Corporal, "I have been sent from Gütersloh to pick up your parachute elastic."

"How much do you need, Sir?

"All of it."

"All of it, Sir?"

"Yes please."

He went away and came back with the Stores Officer who demanded, "Who the bloody hell do you think you are?"

"I am sorry Sir, but I have been sent by Sqn Ldr Lambert, from 16 Squadron, to pick up all your parachute elastic on the orders of the Air Commodore, Lord Bandon." He grumbled, but they fetched a bundle of elastic which he flung down on the table and got me to sign for it. Not a very welcoming chap at all. I waited overnight for the fog to clear and then went back to Gütersloh.

The technical staff had welded little rings on to the wing tips of some Vampires and these rings were joined by three metre lengths of this elastic. The three planes just lined up with the rubber on the ground until they lifted their noses and off they went in tight formation together. The fourth behind, making up the diamond pattern, was not attached on elastic of course.

This stunt was planned for the Farnborough Air Show but it was not to be. The team consisted of Lambert up front and his two wing men were the current Flight Commanders Willie Wilson and Simmy Simpson. Flt Lt Jimpy Shaw was at the back, taking the place of Bob Forester, a very likeable little chap who had recently been killed.

I was watching as they were taking off in a "finger four" formation (think the four nails on your hand), and Bob at the back was due to slide across into the box as soon as possible. He was getting into position, tucking in below the Boss, but it seems he hadn't allowed for the crosswind that pushed the Boss's slipstream straight under him. He had no lift, so down he went to hit the deck, cartwheel and boom. His wife had come out two weeks prior and was there at the time, poor girl. We took his body to the crematorium with no flowers, just greenery: horrible bare, dark green foliage. That was where I grew to hate German Crematoria where I had to attend six times in only eight months.

Back to the elastic Farnborough display. The team was on its way, flying over the North Sea at 25,000 feet, when the Boss started to lose height. They all had to stay with him in formation, but when they asked him why he was descending they got no response on the R/T. By the time they got down to about 8,000 feet with no explanation, Willie and Simmy thought, "Bugger this! If he is going in the drink, we aren't!" They broke away from formation to snap the elastic.

There is an oxygen economiser in the cockpit that manages the air supply. You breathe in through one flap and breathe out of another to have a steady flow in your mask. They think the Boss's economiser had got stuck, cutting his oxygen, so he blacked out at that altitude and slumped forward a bit. This pushed the stick forward to cause a descent. By the time he got down to about 6,000 feet there would have been enough oxygen for him to come round to his senses, so he was able to talk back to the team and carry on flying. By then the elastic was gone, of course, and the spectacle had been ruined. They didn't even go to the air show at all and simply landed at nearby Odiham instead. The Air Officer Commanding, Commodore the Lord Bandon and his assistant, WAAF Sergeant Mollie Grimwood, were waiting at Farnborough in vain to distribute leaflets, telling all about the "tied together display team from 16 Squadron"!

As well as losing Bob Forester there were three more losses in the next six months. One new boy disappeared altogether and he was missing for a long time. We went out searching for a pile of smoking wreckage and found nothing. Several weeks later a farmer phoned to say he had found an aircraft in the forest with the pilot still inside it. It was somewhere near the Minden Gap, a gap in the hills that Hitler's autobahn went through. You could fly through there safely if you aimed for the middle and stayed there. We were banned from there after a time, on the grounds that it was too risky, but I think it was more a case of us upsetting the car drivers going through the gap below us!

Echelon Starboard formation, ready to peel away

We used to practise gunnery and rocketing attacks on the barges along the Dortmund-Emms canal and others. We took great delight in this! I was diving down on a barge one day where a chap was standing at the back. I swooped over very low, literally a few feet over his head, and the poor bugger fell in the water. He obviously complained as we got notification that we were not allowed to attack barges on the canals. We still flew low over them, though, as it was good attack practice and always funny.

112

German farmers used to claim for cows giving birth too early, chickens going off the lay and other livestock issues wherever they thought they could get some compensation out of the Forces.

I started my tale with mention of V for Victor to whet the reader's appetite. We didn't have a particular aircraft allocated to us but ended up flying some much more than others. E-Easy was one I liked, and L-Love was my favourite, I don't know why. (The names usually came from the phonetic alphabet of the time which was the RAF radiotelephony spelling alphabet.)

I was lumbered with V-Victor a fair bit when it had this worrying vibration. I hit a hawk one day at about 2,000 feet. It was hell of a shock for me and of course there were blood and feathers everywhere.

On the day of the rocketing incident at Nordhorn... well, I'm still here, aren't I? Everything settled down and when I got back to base everything was normal for landing. It turned out only to be a short circuit on the rocket switch, but the pyrotechnics inside the cockpit were impressive and gave me one hell of a fright!

As I have said, part of the worry was that V-Victor had been playing up with a strange vibration, and I was not happy with it. I had spoken to my ground crew who had carefully checked over the engine, and could find nothing wrong, and it certainly ran up smoothly and was fine on the ground. I said it was still not right, and I know they were starting to wonder if I was suffering from nerves and simply imagining problems that weren't there.

It was my good luck there was a de Havilland engineer visiting our Squadron just after that incident. We had the oldest Vampires still in service, and amongst other things he was here to check the main wing spars that were all rippled but still safe to fly.

The ripples were caused by pulling heavy g-forces. Boss Lambert was a very good Squadron Leader and we tried many different tactics. If an enemy got behind you, you would call "Break, break!" then go, breaking away to the side. The Vampire was able to turn very tightly and quickly but those manoeuvres always put a lot of stress on the wings.

Our Chief Engineer, or "Chiefy", was Sgt Harry Copley from Yorkshire. He suggested I speak to the de Havilland man about my vibration. When I described the symptoms to this chap he knew what the problem was straight away as he had come across it before. There is a little camera hole in the nose of the Vampire that could take in a little piece of fluff or debris, which made the diaphragm inside act like a Kazoo! In my case, there was a piece of my splattered hawk inside the hole. I was quite surprised, and also very relieved, as it meant that my ground crew went back to believing in me again and V-Victor was no longer a worry to fly.

E -Easy showing her rockets

My first flight commander when I arrived was Dave Ward, DFC, an ex-Spitfire pilot and a damned good bloke. He had great big hands like a farmer. After a few months, 16 Squadron moved from Gütersloh to RAF Celle alongside 93 Squadron. We flew in formation to Celle and met the thickest cloud I had ever flown in. I could just see the trailing edge of Dave's starboard wing. Joe Green was sitting on his port wing. I could gradually see Dave disappearing, just keeping sight of his aileron, but I stuck close to that and managed to follow his movements. I couldn't see my own wingtips, only a couple of feet away from his, and just hoped they wouldn't touch. I found out later that Joe had already pulled away to break formation as he didn't like it one bit.

We came out of the cloud safely and after we landed together Dave said, "God, I didn't realise you were still there!"

I replied, "I didn't want to lose sight of you!" I would have been disorientated and it would have taken me quite a few dangerous seconds to switch back to flying by instruments.

Each Vampire squadron had at least one Meteor, a two-seater, that we used for instrument flying practice. The pilot doing the practice would sit behind with black screens pulled up so he had no possibility of seeing anything. This simulated flying blind and coping with anything: a spin, a black night, filthy weather, iced up windows and so on. The second pilot in the front seat could watch out to make sure all was going well and could interject or take over if necessary.

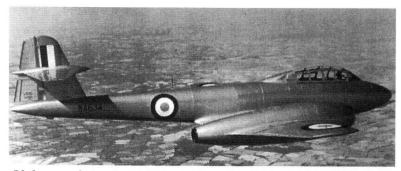

If the weather was bad like that you could call for a GCA (Ground Control Approach) landing. That was a bit rough in those days and not always accurate. They could tell from radar or a DF loop your height and position and talk you down. I did dozens of those as I often flew in bad weather.

Every 600 flying hours the Vampire was taken to bits and put back together at the Advanced Servicing Flight on the airfield. One day at 12 o'clock the Boss said to me, "Geordie, go over to ASF. Pick up J-Jig, give her a fifteen minute air test, then you can go off to lunch."

Great, I thought, that's my lunch hour gone! I had to get over there, sign the forms, then get up in the air, fly around, come down, fill in another form and return to the Mess. That was easily an hour without me getting any grub!

Normally you trusted ASF implicitly. If they said it was okay, then it was okay. On this occasion I went to meet the Corporal and told him I was here to test J-Jig.

115

"Yes Sarge, it's all ready to go."

I signed the Form 700 and walked over to climb in, but something made me walk round the kite. There on the tail plane was the elevator, standing by itself with 32 screws next to it. I would never have made it.

I looked for the Corporal and said, "You told me this is fit to fly? Well come and have a look."

When he saw the state of it, his face went tomato red. "Oh Lord, I know what went wrong. There was an electrician looking at the tail light, and the fitter doing the elevator..."

Each should have finished his job. The electrician had done his bit, and left it for the fitter without telling him, whilst the fitter assumed the electrician had finished it, but it wasn't his job - demarcation.

I said, "There is no way I can take that today."

"I don't know what to say, Sir."

"Well you go and find that bloody electrician and tell him he is lucky not to be on a charge," I said as I went off. Not only was I still alive, but I got my lunch after all.

I was tall and thin (about 6 foot 1 inch but quite a bit shorter these days) and I certainly wouldn't have made a jockey. I was half a head or more taller than many of the other pilots. It was a bit of a squeeze for me in the cockpit of the Vampire which was fairly cramped even for smaller men. I don't think that aircraft won any awards from us pilots in the ergonomics department, but it made up for it in being a joy to fly.

When in my flying suit I was unable to contort my arms enough to hold the high-pressure fuel cock with my left hand and start the engine on the button with my right, like most of the others did. Instead, I had to cross my arms over and do the fuel with my right hand on the left-hand side whilst I operated the starter button with my left hand on the right-hand side.

Early on in my time at Gütersloh we did a quick take off drill. I pressed the starter, and instead of a Goblin engine roaring into life, there was a dull thud then a funny whooshing sound.

My little Corporal on the ground said, "That will cost you a fiver, Geordie!"

Then I realised what I had done. Sadly, the design of the Vampire had the fire extinguisher button right next to the start button, and with my crossed over hands (my forefinger in the position of my second finger) my brain somehow managed to press the wrong one.

Red button, left, is extinguisher
White button next to it is starter

I swore as I climbed out and missed the exercise. I had to see Boss Lambert, who was very decent about it, just saying, "Now you know about it, you won't do it again, will you."

"No, Sir," I agreed.

The ground crew had to take the engine out, clean all the foam out and reinstall it.

But a couple of weeks later, I did the very same thing again. This time the Boss said, "Now, I know how easy it is. But you really are *not* going to do this any more?"

"No Sir, I promise!" And it never did happen again. He was an extremely good boss. He could have torn my bollocks off, but he was very reasonable.

The same could not be said of my new Flight Commander on A flight, Flight Lieutenant Aubrey Covington, after Dave Ward had been posted away. I found Covey increasingly hard to respect as he was a poor leader and a useless navigator. One day, he went too far.

Four of us went off on a big square trip at low level, which burns up jet fuel very quickly. I always kept an air plot in my mind so that I knew where I was. He didn't seem to do that sort of thing, and I have no idea what he relied on. On a square trip, if you do four legs of the same distance at the same speed you end up back where you started, all things being equal. But they usually are not equal, as you do need to take into account the wind, which Covey apparently didn't. It held us back on the way out and sped us up on the return leg so we ended up several miles from where we would have been without any wind.

I could see the airfield lights in the mist way over to our left. "Base to port, 9 o'clock," I said on the R/T. No reply. I repeated it. He was the leader, allegedly, and I was number four in the finger four formation, so I was correcting a lot more than the others and using even more fuel. (In fact, I think I was generally heavier on the throttle than the other pilots anyway, as I did tend to run out quicker at the best of times.)

Covey carried on regardless as he clearly didn't know where he was. I said. "I am getting low on fuel, Covey". There was no helpful answer, just "Stick with the formation, Geordie."

I was hopping mad with him as he was pressing on in the wrong direction, and I was getting desperately short of fuel, so I peeled off and was going to risk landing with the wind instead of against it as normal. I had ten minutes flying time left, at the very most. I came round, and as I was approaching, he had finally cottoned on and had begun turning the rest of them in for landing. As he had a formation of three he took precedence over me, so the tower told me I must go round again. So I was stymied, mentally chewing my fingernails, as I had to slide on over and turn to tack on to the back of them.

We had five fuel gauges. Two went down first, then the second pair, and the last one is saying you are running on hot air. As we came round for landing my last fuel gauge was ticking on nought, so I thought, "Oh blimey, I might not make it!"

I held the nose up in case I had to glide it in for the last 100 yards or so but thankfully I touched down still under power. We got out of the planes, and I went over and said to Covey, "You bloody well nearly run me out of fuel there!"

He was shocked that I was swearing at him, and said, "You come and see me in my office."

"Gladly!" I snapped, as I stalked off.

In his office, I laid into him. "You're no bloody good as a flight commander, you had no idea where you were on this navigation exercise. I could see the airfield when you were quite lost but you wouldn't listen to me!" I was getting redder and redder with anger, the second time in my career that I got hoity-toity with an officer.

He said, "I will put you on court martial!"

"You can bloody well do what you like," I said, as I stormed out.

He reported me to our CO, Boss Lambert, who called me in and asked, "What's all this about, Geordie?"

118

"To be honest Sir, Covey didn't know where he was. I was almost out of fuel and he would not listen. I was close to having to force land because of him."

All he said was, "Would you like to move your kit to B flight with Mr. Philips?"

Phil, the other new Flight Commander, was a good, sensible pilot so I had no hesitation and great enthusiasm in saying, "Yes please, Sir!" and that was the end of the drama.

Dave, Simmy and Phil were a good laugh whereas Covey didn't know what a joke was. I don't know how Covey got to where he was. Someone said he had been a Battle of Britain pilot but I couldn't see him lasting five minutes! Much later on I heard that during the war he was on a flight to the Isle of Man. Navigation errors in bad weather got him lost and he force-landed in the Irish Republic where he went into the Curragh POW camp! I was not surprised.

On Coronation day, after I had left the RAF, there was a flypast organised over the Palace and Covey navigated a flight there from Odiham and I heard from Bysshe Shelley that he made a balls-up of that as well.

My call sign was "Liner One Nine". We did not use plane call signs, it was the pilot's sign, and it didn't matter what plane they were in. When you wanted a homing if you got lost, which wasn't often for me, you would just choose a channel, hit the button and simply say "Liner One Nine" and the base would give you a bearing. "Liner One Nine, steer 310". A man sitting in a cabin had a direction finder (DF) on the radio signal, and his information would go straight through to the tower. I expect Covey was on to that all the time if he was out on his own!

I was a very good shot and was on the Gütersloh Station Rifle Team. We used .303 rifles which I was good with, and also not bad with a pistol unlike most of the others who found that more difficult.

We were going to shoot at Bad Lippspringe in the inter-base rifle competition at 600 and 1,200 yards. We had our own rifles all zeroed ready and took them to the armoury, where the armourer stowed them in a special rack marked "Rifle Team". When we came to collect them on the day, they were gone! We never found out where or why, so we were issued with stock rifles which were un-zeroed. Those distances took some shooting, so we didn't have a chance and didn't shoot at all well which was most disappointing for all concerned.

Gutersloh Rifle Team 1950. The cameraman cut off Ollie Burton, then two men I can't remember, PG Smith, Johnny Veal and me (a PIV)

Another pastime was gliding. With my mates Peter Clayton and Ronnie Queen, who were on 3 Squadron at the same airfield, we were very keen on gliding at the local club which was free for aircrew. Our instructor was an ex-Junkers 88 pilot who was very keen to train us. In the first trainer aircraft we tried out there were no frills whatsoever. You just sat on the wooden seat and had a stick and pedals, no instruments, and just the wind past your ears to judge your speed. It was pure flying and really good fun. I would have liked to have done more of it but there was no opportunity to do so when I was posted away.

At the eastern end of the runway at Gütersloh there was a huge mound of earth and I was told that was Russian prisoners who had been worked to death building the runway and were mass buried there. Whether that tale was based on any truth, I don't know.

Chapter 17
Meeting Mollie

One day we went to the 2nd Tactical Air Force HQ at RAF Sundern which was a complex of administrative buildings just on the other side of Gütersloh.

As new postings we were taken to meet the AOC (Air Officer Commanding), Air Commodore Percy Bernard, the Earl Bandon. I was very nervous, never having been with such a high-ranking person before, but he made us all feel very at ease with his jovial welcome.

By his right-hand side was a WAAF Sergeant called Mollie Grimwood. She looked very glamorous to me with a lovely bubble cut to her hair. I looked at her several times and thought, "Very nice!" but I also reasoned there was no chance of getting off with her. I regretfully thought, "I bet she belongs to some lucky Wingco!"

Mollie didn't like having her photo taken, and wouldn't often smile, so my choice is sadly limited

It turns out I was wrong, as I found out a couple of nights later when most of our squadron attended a 2TAF dance.

For a few months after I was posted to Germany I drank too much alcohol, egged on by the others. I went berserk with my pals Ronnie and Pete when we first arrived. We looked at the card in the Mess and saw that each drink was only 3d or 6d. So cheap! We went down through the card trying them all and at the end of the first night we were well and truly sozzled.

When the older chaps on 16 Squadron realised I was not a drinker they made sure I had plenty more than I could take. I can remember on the evening of that dance they had plied me with plenty of whisky.

I was watching a woman dancing in a delightful black taffeta dress. When she stopped she happened to walk off the dance floor to exactly where I was. I don't know if that was fate or what, but it was Mollie. I asked her for a dance and when we came back off the floor, I was enthralled and at a loss just what to say. So I asked if she'd like a cup of coffee. I brought it back to her, but as I'd had so much to drink I managed to trip and clumsily spill it on her lovely new dress!

Mollie found it hard to know what I was saying, with my Geordie accent, but she found that funny. She thought that I was a bit weird but somehow didn't seem to mind. I took her handbag and remember I had it hanging round my neck. I didn't smoke, but she did and I was dishing out her cigarettes to all and sundry! When we said goodnight I apparently agreed I would ring her in the morning.

We went back to the Mess where I was given yet more whisky until I was absolutely paralytic for the only time in my life. I had little idea what was going on except to vaguely recall a circle of them pushing me around calling out "Timber!" as they shoved me from one side to the other. Two blokes, probably not much more sober than me, had to half-carry me back to my quarters and they decided that, to save walking, we should cross the Holy Acre, which was a big fenced grass area outside the guardroom. My friends took me to the fence, bundled me over, climbed over themselves, walked me across to the next fence, bundled me over that and took me to my room. I started getting undressed, standing on my bed with a big smile on my face and trying to get my trousers off, and the last thing I remember was the radiator coming up to hit me. I was out for the night and don't know how the blow didn't kill me. That was some first date!

Funnily enough when I woke up the next day, to find myself half-dressed with my socks still on, I felt fine other than a bruised head. I was called to the phone and it was Mollie. "You said you would ring me today?" I said I was sorry that I had not yet got round to it. In fact I had totally forgotten that I'd said I would phone her because I had become so drunk.

I asked her, "Would you like to meet down town? WOs and Joes Club in Gütersloh at 7 pm?"

We both cycled in the couple of miles from either direction to meet at the club where we had a bite to eat and a Cassis mixed with lemonade, and then did the same again most nights for months. Mollie had just thought I was a bit strange and I was very lucky she agreed to go out with me after my first performance. I never regretted it, anyway! Having a girlfriend kept me away from the bad influences in the Sergeants' Mess, and that was the end of my drinking days.

Mollie outside the Sundern Sergeant's Mess

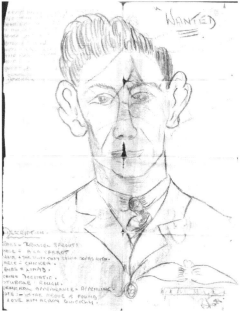

How one of Mollie's best friends saw me as a potential suitor!

WANTED
Ears: brussel sprouts
Nose: a la carrot
Hair: the stuff they stuff sofas with
Neck: chicken
Eyes: Limpid
Chin: Dogmatic
Stubble: rough
General appearance: appealing

NOTE :- If the above is found, lose him again quickly

We both had a few days off in June for some Continental leave. We took a train up to Scharbeutz, on the Baltic coast north of Lubeck, which was a holiday resort for the Forces with a fine beach. There were separate WAAF and Airmen hostels so we stayed apart but met up each morning.

We took a walk in the woods one day where we sat down for a bit of a kiss and cuddle. I saw something out of the corner of my eye. Somebody was watching! I could see it was a Transport Warrant Officer, rather like a Forces train guard. He had followed us and was spying on us to make sure we weren't having a bit of nookie! Which we didn't, as we were not yet married. I was in love and treated her like the lady she was.

On that lovely beach on the Baltic Sea they had big basket seats dotted all around that you could sit in to shelter from the strong sun.

Near the end of our stay I took Mollie out in a kayak for over two hours with my shirt off in which time I got badly sunburned. I dare not report sick as it was a self-inflicted injury, so for over a week I had to suffer in silence as I pulled my shirt over my raw back and climbed gingerly into my flying suit.

After a year I asked Mollie if she would marry me. She agreed, so when we could both get leave together we went to Ipswich where I asked her father for his permission and he also agreed.

We got married on 10th February 1951 at St Mary Stoke church, Ipswich. I had asked a few people who might be suitable as my best man, and who was still alive, but it was hard to find someone available with leave at the right time.

I liked Bob Sowery, a Sergeant Pilot like me at Celle (I think with 93 Squadron) who was a man of the world. He took his leave and drove all the way from Hertfordshire in a car for the wedding, but afterwards he never really spoke to me again before his Squadron was posted away. I wondered later if perhaps he thought I should have offered him some petrol money or something? I regretted that our relationship hadn't ended more happily.

Sister Ella, Self, Mollie & Bob Sowery

Anyway, the wedding went off well. Mollie and I went to have our first honeymoon night in the Connaught Hotel in London. I thought I'd shave before bed to save time in the morning but I found my shaving kit was missing: the boys had taken it out of my case back in Ipswich for a joke. It was very late but I got dressed and went out to search for a shop. At last in Piccadilly I found a chemist shop that had just closed but I battered on the door till the proprietor kindly opened up to sell me a razor! Then I went to bed at long last and we left early the next morning for Fowey in Cornwall where we had a week's wonderful honeymoon.

I can't remember where this honeymoon shot was taken (ha ha!)

My old best chum Steve (Arthur Stevens), who by that time was a navigator in the Middle East, had recommended that we went to his home town. We had a lovely time staying in the Fowey Hotel except one evening we went out to visit Steve's folks and we got home rather late to find the hotel dark and all locked up. There was no response to our knocking and I even went to a phone box to telephone them but got no reply. I decided I had to break in! I tried several sash windows with my pocketknife until I found one where I could force the catch. I pushed up the window and we climbed in, with difficulty, and didn't realise I had left behind a big footprint on one of their tablecloths.

In the morning at breakfast the manager came over to me and asked, "Did you by any chance have trouble getting into the hotel last night? Would that be your footprint, sir?" I admitted that it was and that we had climbed in the window as everything was locked up. "If sir will look at the noticeboard, he will see that he simply needs to borrow a key if he stays out after 10pm." I hadn't spotted that notice, of course!

At breakfast a great big seagull knocked on the window. We were told that people had got him accustomed to receiving a kipper on request, so we also fed him one. I remarked to the manager that he must be a heavy bird, but he explained that even the largest seabirds are ever so light, only a few ounces, and that did surprise us.

When we got back from honeymoon and returned to Germany we had to live separately and wait to be granted married quarters at RAF Celle, which from November 1950 had been my new posting with 16 Squadron.

Mollie had two older brothers. She told me, "The eldest, Geoffrey, went into the Army. My second brother, Ivan, became a Navy officer and they both did nothing but nag me, saying it would do me good to be in the services. I thought: I am not going for either of their choices, so I signed up for the Air Force in Ipswich."

Just before that, when Mollie was 17 she worked in a café for the Forces, much against her father's wishes, as he was quite right that she would be exposed to many young servicemen! An American officer, a bomb aimer based at Debach near Woodbridge in Suffolk, invited her to see Glenn Miller in 1944 in what turned out to be his last concert, we believe. I was rather envious when she told me of that

127

happy evening before I was on the scene. Glenn Miller had been in England doing broadcasts for the BBC, whose HQ was secretly relocated to Bedford during the war. He was staying in that area before he departed from nearby RAF Twinwood for France but sadly failed to arrive.

Mollie had a good education and learned German at school before she went to secretarial college from which she emerged as a furious typist with something like 120 words per minute shorthand, 80 wpm normal typing. She was posted to the Federal Republic of Germany, initially as Secretary to Group Captain Laurence Sinclair at RAF Wahn where they flew Mosquitos. Then Lord Bandon, the AOC of 2 Group, snaffled her to become his PA at 2 TAF HQ.

Mollie enhanced her command of the German language by adding more colloquial expressions picked up from the many Germans that were employed for all kinds of duties.

Mollie was tied to the AOC and as such was separate from the other WAAFs. She had her own quarters and there was no need to parade with all the others, as she was always by his side. She thought the world of Lord Bandon who was a lovely man, and she guarded him with her soul. She would take the outside office and keep people away, however urgent they thought they were, with "Sorry, but the Air Commodore is asleep."

Lord Bandon had his own Avro Anson plane and his personal pilot named Peter Postlethwaite for routine transport. Whenever he wanted to fly anywhere he would say to Mollie, "Tell P12 to get my plane ready, would you." The first time she had to think hard about what he meant... got it! P followed by 'ostlethwaite' - twelve letters!

The Earl, known as Paddy, was quite a character and he was friends with Richard "Batchy" Atcherley, one of the Atcherley twins who were both pilots. He and Batchy Atchy apparently bricked up the officer's mess one night so the others couldn't get out. Paddy landed a Vampire too fast one day and went through the hedge at the end of the runway. Mollie told me that Batchy had sent him a telegram saying:

CONGRATULATIONS. HEAR YOU HAVE BEEN THROUGH THE BARRIER!

The other Atcherley twin, David, was flying a Meteor from Cairo to Cyprus when he disappeared. I remember reading about that in Air Clues which I always read cover to cover in case I could learn something that might help save me from a similar fate.

Mollie carried on with her work after we married until she was discharged in May 1951. The AOC bought her a silver cigarette case as a thank you present, inscribed:

With best wishes from Air Commodore the Earl Bandon

I never really got to meet him myself, except when I finished in Germany and he asked me what I was going to do next. He spoke very nicely but not posh.

Mollie amongst spectators for a football match
in Hamburg: BAOR versus BAFO

Young Mollie

129

Chapter 18
RAF Sylt weapon training

E ach BAFO Squadron went twice a year to Sylt for weapons training and practice where we stayed about a month each time. We did air firing and rocketing as they had stopped bombing from the Vampire by that time.

With the air-to-air firing on a drogue I got a 22% score which was said to be exceptional, but a day or two later someone else got 23% so my record didn't stay in place for long!

Mollie's mother, Grace, came out for a holiday with us at Sylt. She told us that on her train there was a young pilot with wings who was quite small and only looked about 16. She asked if he was on our squadron to which I replied, "Yes he is. Or at least, he was."

It was tragic. He had only managed to unpack his flying helmet and gloves and he was up in a Vampire to try an attack on the flag. He totally missed it, so when he came down they took him up in a Mosquito to show him how to turn tightly for firing in a curve of pursuit. (We all had an initial go with a pilot attack instructor for half an hour in his "old rattle-banger", as we called his Mosquito, just to tease him.) The young lad got into his Vampire and set up an attack path in what was much too sharp a turn. He stall-turned and flipped into the sea and there he was sixty feet under the waves on his very first day.

Grace found the German shops very interesting. She went into town one day and was getting off the tram when a German woman in front of her turned round and spat right at her feet. She simply lifted her head up high and walked on.

As we were married we stayed at a house in Sylt with a German family who said, "You British are very welcome here, we are nothing to do with the Nazis!" But in the dresser drawer there was some newspaper lining, which Mollie lifted to give it a shake out, and underneath was a long-overlooked picture of the man of the house in a Nazi uniform, complete with Swastika. We did not let on that we had rumbled his dirty secret.

130

We managed a bit of R & R on the weekends spent at Sylt

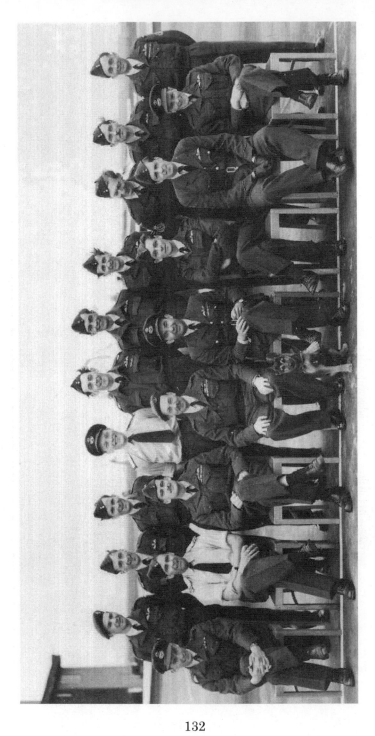

132

Sylt Group APS May 1951.

Back row, L-R:

1. Joe Green (Cody's owner)
2. "Ace" MacKenzie who knew it all 3. Another "Ace", Greg
4. George Morris. National Service nice lad.
5. Me - who needed a haircut, then?
6. Slim Holliday   7. Frank Green
8. PG Smith
9. "Bottle Happy" Cliff Metcalf, he liked a drink
10. Wheels Up Ollie

Front Row, L-R

11. Bysshe Shelley   12. Burton
13. Twitch "Covey" Covington (he had a nervous tic)
14. The Boss at this time, Wing Co Sing with Joe's Pooch Cody
15. Flt Lt Al Philips   16 Johnnie Veal -
17. Dickie Peters- nicest of them all
18 Ron Taylor, another young National Service pilot, nice guy.

As well as the targets at Sylt we had a rocketing range at Fassberg. Dickie Peters and I were on a practice together one day. He went to fire off two of his concrete-tipped dummy rockets and then broke away. I heard some strange noises over the R/T and wondered what was going on. I went in and fired my two rockets, and broke away, and heard more noises, so I knew something was not right.

I flew alongside him and said, "Put your fist in the air if everything is OK." He looked over at me, but no fist.

"What's wrong, Dickie?" There was just a rushing noise on the intercom for a reply. I came in tight - we would go within six inches of each other's wings when we wanted to - and I could see his canopy was broken. What had happened was the concrete tip of the practice rockets we used had broken upon firing, and a lump of it had been thrown back and smashed into the canopy. The rushing of wind drowned out his voice over the R/T.

He was climbing away slowly. I said, assuming correctly that he could hear me, "Dickie, I'll take you back, you formate on me." He stayed fairly flat and level, so I guessed there were some other issues. I took a wide bank round which he could follow and he stayed close to me back to the airfield. I carried on over the grass alongside him and, once I was sure he had landed safely on the runway, I went on round again and landed myself. He was very grateful for my assistance.

The reason for his limited manoeuvrability was that a smaller bit of concrete, the size of a finger nail, had lodged in his tail plane so he could not properly move it. If it had jammed in an up or down position he would have gone straight down, or straight up until he stalled and then crashed to the ground. Either way he would be dead as we were at

Dickie Peters with Geordie Bewick

low altitude and the Vampire didn't have an ejector seat!

Another minor rocketing incident for me was at Senelager Ranges near Paderborn. The Vampire seat was adjustable on rails, like in a car, and whilst I was doing an attack the seat latch became unlocked. I was sliding backwards and forwards very violently as I tried to break away after firing the rockets. Most uncomfortable and quite a worry. Once out of the manoeuvre I was able to free a hand to make sure the seat was firmly locked in place!

Joe Green was a strange lad who kept a pet dog on the station, which was not common. Cody spent most of his time at Celle but Joe took him everywhere, including to Sylt.

Joe was usually the last to get up. Cody was awake before him here, giving his ear a wake-up lick!

Lofty Edmunds with Cody at Sylt

Lofty Edmunds was one of the ground crew who kept us safe. He was friendly with the pilots and often in our company as a friend. Some ground crew three-stripers were not so friendly because young pilots were automatically given three stripes with our wings, in considerably less than the time they had taken to earn theirs. (We believe that may be why the 'P' rank system was brought in for a time.)

The stripes were to protect pilots should they be shot down or crash land in enemy territory. In theory you would get some recognition and kinder treatment with a rank, although that didn't always work. An air gunner friend of mine was shot down during the war into the city centre of Essen. He was snagged up on a lamp post when a gaggle of German women came on the scene. They set about hanging him with his own parachute cords from that same post. They were about to haul him up when a German policeman came on the scene and stopped the hanging and took him away as a prisoner. He was most grateful that the policeman behaved as the articles of war prescribed enabling him to finish his war in a POW camp. Not all were so lucky. I believe many were killed by angry women in cities where their homes and shops had been destroyed by our bombs.

Geordie Bewick (I think) in a Meteor

Chapter 19
Weather, a wheels-up landing, and more sad losses

On a typical day we arrived on the airfield at 07:30. There was a meteorological briefing at 7:45. The forecasts were quite poor in those days and not very reliable. If the skies were clear with a reasonable forecast, all well and good. Otherwise, at 08:00 Boss Lambert would usually tell me to go off and check it out. He knew I was keen on weather and would tend to send me up to 30,000 feet to look around for 30 minutes to judge what the weather might do, and report back to the squadron.

This was more risk for me when the weather was no good, but I took every opportunity to fly, including air tests, and hence flew more hours than many of the others. We were able to fly in any weather with our advanced instrument flying rating, but the Vampire was not really equipped for all weather flying and we had no radar.

After my recce we would muster in the crew room and wait for the Flight Commanders to put up some groups, pairs and multiples thereof up to 8, and off we would go to do exercises. We did some sort of task most days. We were supposed to fly a minimum of 30 hours a month to keep our hand in. At one time we were restricted to that as the maximum because of a shortage of budget, we were told. We used up gallons of fuel! The Vampire carried about 330 gallons. We could fly for only about 2.5 to 3 hours through the thin air at high altitude, but at low level this would drop down to only 45 mins. To increase our range we would often carry a 100 gallon drop tank under each wing which meant we could extend our flying times.

If it was terrible weather and there was no special exercise then there would be no flying. Sometimes we watched German wartime reels of their pilots coming up behind the Allied bombers and shooting them down. Just for interest and perhaps to learn something of their tactics. It is not very pleasant to see a stricken bomber peel away and no parachutes coming out. Sometimes, in a spin, the centrifugal force kept the crew pinned tight so they simply could not make their way out.

On what was the old Empire Day, 24th of May, our Adjutant Flt Lt Joe Greenhill came up to me and said we were to go off in Meteor 7 WA.657 to do some conversion flying. I was taken aback as I had already done the Meteor and Vampire course at RAF Driffield and was fully conversant with the Meteor. Joe asked me how many hours had I got on the Meteor? I said something over twenty and Joe revealed he only had ten hours. He asked if I had done single engine landings, and when I said I had, he said could he go and do some of those after some aerobatics. My pleasure!

He signed up as skipper and got in the front seat and I sat in the rear seat. I was right to think he wouldn't need any help with aerobatics, as he would have done plenty of hours on Spitfires and Vampires. Meteors were no different but had two engines of which one might fail, and that was a scenario that needed practice.

I helped him through a couple of single engine approaches where we came in with wheels down as if to land but didn't complete the landing. Instead we carried on round and popped the wheels up ready to practice another. For single engine work you just throttle one engine right back and only use the other one. The dead engine causes drag which you have to correct with your opposite rudder to hold it straight.

On Joe's third attempt there was a red warning light appeared on the starboard wheel. I said. "Don't take any notice of that, that is just micro relay switch trouble, we had a lot of that in England." Famous last words. As we were coming in, we got a call on the radio from the tower" "Are you aware your starboard wheel isn't down?" No, we said. And privately we muttered some other words!

Joe pulled out of the approach and we agreed we would go up to 7,000 feet and do some G-dives to see if we could shake the wheel down. Joe was diving and pulling up sharply and I was pumping the hydraulics but to no avail.

I said "Joe, we are committed to a belly landing. Are you happy to do that?" I was more experienced in this type, but it is much easier to do from the front seat than the back seat. I said, "On the approach you concentrate on the landing, I will look after the low pressure and high pressure cocks and I will jettison the hood just as we cross the airfield boundary."

138

You had to jettison the heavy hood as late as possible as it weighed two hundredweight and, if released at higher speeds, it had been known to take the tail off with tragic consequences.

We came around for the final landing, in a nice steady approach towards the grassed area with the wheels up, and as we crossed the boundary I shut off the fuel cocks and pulled the hood release.

The hood needed a good shove that took some skin off my forearm, enough to hurt. We hit the grass and shot along for several hundred yards with such deceleration that our arms shot out in front of us with nothing to brace against. Instead of the hood going back behind as expected, it was bouncing along beside us. As we came to a halt, the hood did one final bounce over the starboard wing and then that also stopped.

Chiefy Copley told me later that half the station was out watching this action and he added, "Geordie, do you realise that hood could have bounced back into the cockpit?" I said no and was very glad it had never even occurred to me!

The fault was that a tie rod operating the D-door of the starboard wheel bay had not been secured by a piece of copper wire to ensure the male-female joint did not unwind with vibration. The unit was insecure and had unwound ten complete turns over a period of time and then finally separated during our flight. Two penn'orth of copper wire would have prevented this.

The accident was classified "Avoidable accident", Ground crew Error Cat.4 in the BAFO Avoidable Accident Rates. The report said "Good airmanship was shown by Captain and pupil." I had to smile when I realised I was supposed to be the pupil! However, Joe did extremely well in the circumstances and we were both very grateful for it all to end so well. WA 657 suffered little damage and was repaired to fly again right into the late 1960s. The Meteor was a strongly built machine. It was very good to fly too, very stable and went up to about 820mph. I preferred the Vampire which was great to fly acrobatically, although with one engine it had a top speed of only about 560mph. In general, the Meteor Squadrons were based in the UK and the Vampire Squadrons in Germany.

As well as the Meteor being okay, we were both okay as well. It was the case all too regularly that pilots were not so lucky. I seemed to be rather unfortunate in the number of fatal crashes I observed from the ground.

I had come back on leave as spare man sitting on a spare aeroplane, waiting to see if one dropped out of a formation of sixteen. Tubby Valance was Number 8 and his pair took off past me, got airborne, then turned round to join on to their finger four. Tubby went straight past the formation and plonk! Straight into a cornfield, almost as if he intended it. We never had any idea why it happened. The Vampire burst into flames and was buried several feet in the ground. The big engine is right behind you so if you hit the ground and stop suddenly, you are mincemeat.

My leave fell at the wrong time, yet again. I had just come back so I was spare man when we displayed twelve Vampires in tight formation at the 1951 Paris Air Show. The team had flown to Orleans in France with drop tanks full and kept the tanks on for the show. I made my way from Gütersloh to Orleans in an American Fairchild C-82 transport plane which was a twin boom design like the Vampire.

140

I got talking to the pilot and he let me have a go flying that for 30 mins on the way. It was an ungainly thing that wandered all over the sky like a drunken bus.

The Vampire design meant the tail and hence the jet exhaust pointed down on taxi and takeoff. At Orleans the tarmac was laid during the war by Frenchmen for the Germans and, credit to them, they didn't do it very well! We were blowing sheets of it off the runway at times and had to be careful as a lump of it could go in the next plane's engine.

On the day of the show the display team lined up in twos. The Boss and his number 2 went first. He took off and flew up the runway, then a couple of miles ahead he turned back to let the others join up behind him. Ken Ashman was in the last pair and as he took off he immediately started turning. I was watching from the ground and remember thinking, "Oh Ken, don't, don't, don't! You'll stall!" And indeed, down he went and that was the end of him. He was doing a steep turn with not enough speed for the extra weight of those large tanks. (Prince William of Gloucester did exactly the same with a small craft in 1972 when he turned too soon.) You need plenty of engine power and speed before you bank sharply or you will fall out of the sky.

It was too late in the schedule for me to have time to get up and catch the formation so they carried on and did the show with one

plane short. I wondered if any of the crowd would notice and question why?

It was one of the Flight Commanders, either Simmy Simpson or Willie Wilson, who when I first arrived on squadron had just had a major crash. He was coming into land where you normally have ten to fifteen degrees of flap on and in the final approach you go full flap. He didn't select the flap as he hit the dive brakes by mistake! This instantly cut his speed so he stalled and cartwheeled... but he walked out of that with only a scratched ankle, which is amazing when you look at the state of the cockpit. No idea how he got away with that. For many pilots they make just one little mistake and that's it...

Willie became a Squadron Leader and when I was up at Acklington in the UK he brought a squadron of Meteors there and it was good to see him again.

My pal Ginger Sharp from Cannock came on to fly Vampires in Germany and on one steep dive he burst his eardrum which grounded him for six months. As soon as it was repaired he went back flying, I think from RAF Wunstorf, and I was told that on his first trip whoever was leading the formation took them at a low-level sweep, literally at the tree tops, and Ginger clipped a tree with his wing. That spun him round and down he went, boom, and that was it. As I have said he was very sharp by nature and I was surprised he got caught out by that, but it was always potentially lethal following tightly behind someone who does not necessarily allow for your different altitude in the formation.

142

Chapter 20
Operation Rainbow and Americans

T he Americans invited 16 Squadron to go down to stay at Rhein-Main Air Base in the US Zone to take part in Operation Rainbow in September 1950. (I could have known about this before my CO did, as Mollie was sitting on the right-hand side of the AOC. She knew exactly what was going on everywhere, long before the squadrons did! But she kept "mum".)

Crew Room with 16 Squadron at Rhein-Main Air Base in the American Zone for Operation Rainbow 1950.
Standing: Simmy Simpson, Johnny Veal, Ollie Burton, Joe Greenhill.
Sitting: Aubrey Covington, can't remember, Dickie Peters, Self, Jock Reid, Frank Green, James "Bysshe" Shelley, Richard "Greg" Gregory, PG Smith, Ollie the Pole

I will digress and mention a bit about these men, as I remember them.

Simmy Simpson (B Flight commander at that time) was a jovial chap with a DFC from Spitfires and a "let's go get 'em!" attitude. One time he came back with a branch embedded in his wing tip, so he was clearly flying very low! I loved the guy as a flight leader. His wife was a lady with money, I believe, as she bought him a motorcar. He was racing around the roads of Germany until he crashed and wrote it off.

Johnny Veal had a reputation for landing too fast. That meant the heat of the brakes could be too much for the inner tubes of the tyres. "Bang! Bang!" - that's Johnny arriving!

Ollie Burton I didn't know well as I didn't do much with him, but I think he became a flight commander.

Joe Greenhill was the adjutant who did the wheels-up Meteor landing with me. As he was commissioned as a Flight Lieutenant he hung out at the Officers' Mess so we didn't mix much but we were still very friendly.

Covey I have mentioned! The worst flight commander I ever came across with no idea how to find his way or lead anything.

Dickie Peters was a lovely fellow. A real gentleman and a great pilot. He took me with him when he could, as he knew I had excellent eyesight. There was a famous chap called Group Captain John "Catseyes" Cunningham who shot down a lot of enemy at night. The story going around during the war was that the best night fighters were eating a lot of carrots, as they were good for the eyesight and helped you see in the dark. A lot of baloney that still persists to this day! It was in fact a cover story for the new radar in the Bristol Beaufighter night-fighters. Incidentally Cunningham became a test pilot at de Havilland and took a Vampire up to 59,000 feet for the altitude record. God knows how he got it up there, as we could only get up to about 40,000 feet.

Anyway, I hadn't a particular appetite for carrots myself, but I had very good eyesight that was better than most. I could see ten miles easily on a bright day. Dickie must have told the CO that "Geordie is eagle-eyed," as Boss Lambert and his successor both selected me as their No 2 to stick with them in combat if the Russians started any trouble. No 2 sticks by the tail of No 1 to cover him, but there was nobody protecting poor No 2...

Jock Reid was posted away to 14 Squadron not long after this exercise so I didn't really get to know him. He was very experienced and maybe 14 Squadron needed that to bolster their skills at the time.

Frank Green was a nice enough lad, from Jersey, although he did seem to go on about the delights of his home country a lot! I gather it's a lovely holiday destination.

James "Bysshe" Shelley was a young pilot officer. He was a happy lad with the nicest smile of anyone I ever knew, and I did like him, even though he was very pushy and keen to get promoted. I don't blame him for that, and I think he made Wing Co, although he was nothing special at flying. Like Covey, he always wore a peaked cap; it was below their dignity to wear a beret or forage cap! He was Covey's protégé and was always given the plum jobs. The rough jobs came to Sergeant Pilots like me, but I didn't mind one bit as I loved flying and went up as often as possible.

This Officer and NCO situation was one of the banes of my RAF career. At the time I went in, the RAF were doing things on the cheap. Half of every squadron was made up of NCO pilots, the other half were made up to Officers. Bysshe came through on the course behind me at Cottesmore, just when they changed the system. From that intake onwards they were all commissioned. It really was not fair and that hurt me deeply, not least in my pocket as they were paid more for doing the same!

I flew with Greg several times but I considered him a conceited little bugger, as I always hated a know-all. Anything about flying he knew, which maybe he did, but it's not as if nobody else on a fighter squadron would know as well! (Some of us nicknamed the big-headed boys as "Ace", out of their hearing, with considerable irony.)

PG Smith was a weird character but a brilliant pilot. He would never polish his buttons. Everyone else would rigorously polish for a funeral or a big parade, but his buttons remained green as he simply wouldn't do it. He almost never said a word, except he did like driving Morgan cars and that is something he would talk about if you let him get on the subject. When flying he liked to use the old-fashioned hand signals from the First World War. He wouldn't use the intercom, which was not always very helpful! He had been a Spitfire Ace in Burma. I heard a story that he had been over Cardigan Bay off Wales, leading a four of pupils, and his Wing Co dived down on him, chopped his tail off, and he went in the drink. I can't be sure that is correct.

145

PG was an excellent aerobatic pilot and he was chosen to do a display for the AOC's inspection. Mollie was with the Earl of Bandon out on the airfield when PG did his practice. He was doing his figure of eights in his Vampire and went down in a spin, falling out of sight behind some trees and they were just waiting for a bang and the smoke when, from over these trees, out shot PG at great speed. Quite brilliant!

Ollie the Pole was a nice Polish chap, obviously! He became known as "Wheels Up" Ollie, because on take off one day he tried to get his wheels up too early when they were still touching the ground, and his Vampire dropped down onto the runway (but was not a write off). Some people could time it just right and select wheels up just as they lifted off. Ollie thought he had mastered that when clearly he hadn't!

Back to Operation Rainbow itself in the US Zone of South Germany. We held the north and were acting as the enemy to test the US defences. We never met their fighter pilots who we were dog-fighting with as they were based at Furstenfeldbruck, whilst for the exercise we were based at Rhein-Main, near Frankfurt. This had two runways; the one to the north was civilian, the one to the south was used by a US MATS (Military Air Transport Squadron) from where we operated.

Self during Operation Rainbow

We flew down there with drop tanks on, landed on the military runway, taxied up and parked up. We always took our ground crew with us on Ops and they followed on in a Dakota or other transport aircraft. The Americans provided bowsers to refuel our planes.

On our first morning I was the first up in the air because Boss Lambert said, as usual, "Off you go, Geordie. Ghastly day, weather check please."

I did my ground checks, started the engine up and all was well. So off I rolled to the runway. The engine should run up to 10,200 revolutions per minute (rpm) to give the power needed for take-off. I wondered what was going on when I found I could not get above 9,400 rpm. Perhaps surprisingly, those last few revs are the ones that give the biggest push and they were vital! I was half way down the runway with the revs still not coming up and I didn't think I would lift off. The trees were looming fast, too late to abort, so I yanked her off the ground and just made it, pretty much scraping the tree tops, and it frightened the life out of me for a moment.

I climbed to 30,000 feet and flew round a bit, and the aircraft behaved perfectly well. I found much of the sky thereabouts was a mass of cloud. I landed and told the Boss it was pretty claggy but we'd seen worse. I also told him about the strange problem I had had getting the revs up, so he got Chiefy to look over my engine. Everything seemed quite normal.

After briefings the Boss went to take off leading his four and they experienced the same thing, with no revs above about 9,400. I watched as he brushed the tree tops and the others followed him in similar fashion as they all made it up safely.

While they were out and about our brilliant ground engineers were looking into the problem and they worked out that the American fuel, JP4, was not the same as our Avtur paraffin which is purer. Our engines were not taking kindly to their stuff. We also later realised that was why the American jet engine exhausts smoked so much, whilst ours burned cleaner. We just had to learn to fly with their fuel whilst we were down there.

It was a very interesting time staying in the US Zone. When we went to our cookhouse we had been used to a little bit of butter, a little sugar, and generally sparse meals. Britain was still under rationing in 1950 and they passed the shortage on to us too. (The officers would have done better, no doubt, but not us NCO pilots.) Here in the US Zone they provided cornflakes and every morning we were offered a quart (two pint) bottle of milk. The first day I said, "I only need to cover my cornflakes," but the cook said, "Take it, if you want it, and drink the rest." So I did, with gratitude.

I asked him how they managed to do it. He said their transport squadron flew in fresh milk from Holland every morning. There were rolls galore. Butter for them? Help yourself as much as you like! When we were given chicken for dinner it was not a mere slice, it was half a bird. They had bananas and oranges which we never got to see ourselves. The Americans always fed their troops very well, and very wise too.

Posing for an official photo by the American Forces,
with navigation maps in my pocket

Each night one of us had to be Duty Pilot in the CCC (Combined Communications Centre). There, you had to sit and wait all night for a piece of paper on the fax machine, which would eventually come in at any hour with directions that the CO of each of the squadrons had to take as a result of the staff meetings. When I was on duty I had to deliver a message somewhere, and on arrival I met a lady soldier on duty. She pointed her rifle at me and yelled. "Halt! Who goes there?"

"Friend," I answered, "Royal Air Force."

"Where's your ID?"

I had my Form 1250 (ID Card) in my pocket and held it up so I could show her my mug shot.

She said, "Put it on the ground! Step back and lie down!"

She looked at it then looked at me, and said "Okay, you can get up." They took security very seriously! We did too, with RAF police and dogs patrolling, but not to those extremes. Whilst we were there a sentry on the perimeter shot dead a German civilian who was trying to climb in for some reason. They didn't mess about asking questions.

On the Operation Rainbow exercise the idea was for us to attack their area, dogfight with them and try to shoot them down with camera guns, which we did with regular success. For operations we did not take any notice of the routine Squadron Flights and the usual flight commanders. I looked on the board one morning and there's my name. I'm No 4 with Simmy. So that should be fun!

Off we went to invade the Americans and we came up behind four F84s. The US pilots were rather careless, we thought, always chatting and not watching what was going on. Simmy broke away from us and went after the leader. He came screaming up behind him and got his camera gun on him and was intending to pull up above him, but their leader happened to come up at the same time too, so Simmy had to yank up his kite very severely. So much so that both his fuel drop tanks fell off his wings! The tanks were only held on with a half-inch bolt, and the g-force was enough to rip them off. (That would leave a pipe flailing and just a small loss of fuel.) Simmy could deal with it all, no bother, as he took risks all the time.

I was watching from behind and when I saw those tanks flying off I thought for a moment they had collided, and it was all over for Simmy, but he got away with it as usual. Some of us got (camera)

149

shots in on the other planes in the US group whilst all this was going on.

Most airfields had a caravan to supervise take-off and landing to assist the tower from a different aspect. They were equipped with a Very cartridge gun to launch a red flare if someone was too high or low to let them know they should go round again. One American shot himself in the control caravan and we had no idea why.

Cliff "bottle happy" Metcalf (he liked his drinks and smokes!) was a character. We weren't allowed to go into Frankfurt, that was out of bounds, but he and I got a lift down in a lorry to visit the local town of Darmstadt. When we got there, we realised it had been heavily bombed (subjected to a firestorm attack in 1944) but some of the shops were functioning. We went down the Main Strasse to look at what they had for sale when we realised that there were people collecting behind us, and in some numbers. We realised how much the place had been knocked about by our lot and that we were not safe to be there in our pilot's uniforms.

"This is looking ominous," I said to Cliff, "When I say go, let's dive down that side street!" We pretended to keep on looking in windows until we shot off, running like hell. We found the main road and hitched a ride back to base.

At the end of the exercise General John Cannon, a small man with piercing blue eyes, came into our crew room to see us. He said, "I want to congratulate you guys for shooting down all my planes. Well done! Now I am going to speak to my guys and kick their asses."

I liked the Americans, in general, as they tended to be jovial, talkative and generous. When we were at Cannock, Woody and I befriended a tough looking soldier in the local tea shop named Delbert Scott Jensen. Before he was drafted he had been a travelling horseback carpenter in Utah, making enough to live on if he slept in barns. He was a friendly guy who got wounded soon after landing in France, as he told me in a letter. I never heard from him again and only hope he made it home from the infantry.

We had Major Jabara, one of the first American jet aces, come to Gütersloh to give us a lecture about the Korean War. He had a big moustache and what he told us was very interesting. They had hand-held radios, which we hadn't got, so if you were shot down in the jungle you could get help. "It's a little device the size of a cigar case, that's a radio and how good the technology is now. When your support guys get a bearing on you from the radio they send in an egg whisk - that's a helicopter - to pick you up."

The losses were quite high, as the MiG-15 was as good or better than their F-86 Sabres, but of the planes shot down he said they managed to rescue most of the crew. At the end of the talk he asked for volunteers to join the UN forces, as replacements for those shot down, we supposed! I think pretty much everyone volunteered but in the end they took nobody from Germany, only pilots based in Britain.

The most famous American we met was General Eisenhower. He was NATO Supreme Commander, but he was resigning his post to go back to the States to become President. Different squadrons of various nationalities gathered at RAF Celle to give him a send off. He came to each squadron on parade and shook hands with all the pilots and ground crew and thanked us for supporting NATO. He was a friendly chap who smiled and seemed to mean what he was saying.

I had my camera behind my back and was determined to get his picture. When he finished, he turned to get in his staff car and I lifted my camera to get a shot... but I was too slow and all I got was a blurred photo of his bum!

Probably the worst picture of Ike ever to be published

It was an incredible day with Brits, Norwegians, Swedes, Dutch, Belgian, French and Americans gathered in about 300 aeroplanes. On that day, for Ike's benefit, the Top Brass wanted to demonstrate what would happen if the Russians were coming and they arranged for several squadrons, well over a hundred fighters, to rush to take off together.

A red cartridge was fired from the control tower and we all taxied out of dispersal. We were all in such a hurry that we didn't give time for our ground crew to remove the pitot head covers. (The pitot head is part of the airspeed indicator which is covered up on the ground to stop dirt and dust getting in. With those covers on we would be without the airspeed reading that was so crucial to prevent stalling.) We were surprised to see a car running alongside us with ground crew frantically waving their arms! We stopped and the covers were quickly removed, and on we went as the mad scramble continued and we all took off to fly west. How there was not an almighty coming together, we don't know. Normally one or two took off at a time with a reasonable interval to the next pair, but we were six abreast, roaring down this runway. Those ahead went off in a cloud of dust, we did the same with others following in our dust then fanning off left or right. If anyone had burst a tyre or had any sort of prang there would be one almighty mess as no one could possibly stop when we were all totally committed to getting airborne.

It was very frightening, we all agreed afterwards, and quite unforgettable. It worked, however, and I wish there had been a news reel made of it! All the planes then headed off back to their own countries and bases.

Chapter 21
RAF Celle and the Staines raid

I n November 1950, 16 Squadron was moved to RAF Celle. When some squadrons came out to Germany from England for a detachment the first thing many of the lads did was go down to Hanover to find a brothel. I never was inclined to do that, nor were any of my mates in 16 Squadron. A risky business in several respects!

Celle was only eleven miles from the new border with East Germany, one of the RAF stations closest to the Russians. There was a forest to our east and blocking our view. If the Russians came we reckoned we wouldn't know much about it in advance, and the plan was to abandon the airfield as quickly as possible, flying off west to regroup!

We often flew into East German air space when the wind was from the west, which it tended to be. We often worked to a QGH homing signal to aid our return to base in poor visibility. There was a little radio station with a radio transmitter, but there is no signal directly upwards which is known as the cone of silence. When the signal disappears you know you are over base. At that point you descend from 30,000 ft to 12,000 ft heading east, turn round some miles over the border and come back heading west to land into the wind. (Q symbols were just signifying different codes and the Q didn't actually mean anything.) When the visibility was really bad you requested

GCA approach, but we didn't have those facilities at Celle and would go to other airfields to rehearse that.

Mollie and I had our first married quarters together at Celle. One day, when we were both away at Sylt, a big storm hit the town of Celle and struck our flat with lightning. It blew all the fuses and all the electricity conduits were blown part. An 18-inch square corner was blown off the building which let water pour in throughout. That wrecked the cooker, radio, bed and more besides. Somebody rang up Sylt to leave a message that our flat had been damaged, but there was nothing much we could do about it!

Boss Lambert left our Squadron in 1951 when we had a nice chap called Sing as the new CO for a while. Next was Benwell, all too briefly, as it turns out he had not properly passed his promotion to Squadron Leader or some such. He had to hand over the command and leave which was a shame as he was a good bloke and seemed perfectly able in the job. My fourth and last CO was R U P De Burgh, a bit officious, but perfectly okay.

One job I was given was keeping up to date the pilot's board that held a record of hours, GCAs, rocketing, cannon firing and bombing (before they stopped that).

I was doing a good job of that and one day the Boss said, "The Pilots' Order Book needs sorting out." These were orders and updates from the AOC that apply to everybody, almost like a newsletter with crashes, additions, squadron movements and so on. We all needed to read it to keep up to date. He brought out a thick, scruffy file crammed with papers. He said, "A lot of that stuff is old rubbish now. The old wartime stuff can go." That was real history and how I regretted, in years to come, throwing it all away as instructed.

I went to see a fellow Geordie pal in the workshops and said I need an aluminium cover, back and front, with a squadron badge on it. No problem, he said, and he used a piano hinge to make a folder. The Boss really liked the job we made of it.

On New Year's Eve most of them were drinking copiously, no doubt, but I would be in town with Mollie. We would stay up until midnight at a dance or something, sipping our lemonades!

We were allowed to fly with alcohol in those days, although it was not of course advisable. We used to have a "Wing Ding" on New Year's

154

Day, where we would get all the planes up from the whole Wing flying at low level to cause some noise and annoyance to the locals!

Our Wing comprised 3, 16 and 94 Squadrons, a total of about 48 aircraft. A squadron had 24 planes but at any one time we had about 16 or at the most 20 flying, as we never had them all serviceable.

Our AOC, Lord Bandon, had an inspection every year where we would lay on some displays. I was involved in some elaborate ones in the early 1950s. These pictures show the formations we made up from our Wing. "R" was 94 Squadron, "A" was 16 Squadron where I am flying No 3 as shown, and the "F" was 3 Squadron.

Ralph

These big formations would be plotted out on the ground. There was insufficient space to lay them out on the runways so we just laid out smaller sections which had to be imagined relative to the others. There would be someone flying outside who acted as a whipper in, and obviously we had feedback from the ground too, as we were always in R/T contact together.

On one of the inspections we were visited by the renowned war veterans Lord Tedder, Chief of Air Staff at the time, alongside Air Marshall Thomas "Bill" Williams, Commander in Chief of the British Air Forces of Occupation. Lord Tedder was a very dapper and jovial man who would say things to make us laugh. Bill looked a big bloke alongside him.

A couple of times we flew over to England for an exercise with the Army on Salisbury Plain. The first was to RAF Odiham for Exercise Hotdog and Exercise Kingpin. For these exercises a visiting squadron often had their own temporary runway prepared by an airfield construction unit who laid sheets and sheets of pressed steel plate with holes in it over the grass. This kept us out of the way of the normal airfield traffic.

Sometimes on exercise we were given proper accommodation, and other times we were in temporary tin huts or literally camping in tents. Another unfair inequity here - commissioned pilots tended to get a room and sergeant pilots tended to get a tent!

At Odiham we were camped on the south side of the airfield in a dip past the end of the runway. This put us pretty much out of sight of the control tower and the main part of the station. One day a Lancaster landed and trundled right along to the end of the runway before half turning round, at which point they paused. The door opened and the crew threw out cartons, carpets, silks... all sorts of contraband. After a few words we piled it up for them and after they had parked up their aircraft they turned up with a truck. It would be stuff they had bought in Europe and were avoiding the UK duty.

Another year we had a stay at RAF Filton for Exercise Surprise Packet with the Army on Salisbury Plain. As soon as we touched down from Germany, out from behind the hangars came a string of lorries, with a customs officer on each, and they went to each of our planes and asked what we had brought from Germany. Well, I had brought an umbrella back. There was one circular panel in the wing which you wouldn't notice unless you knew it was there, where I had stowed it safe. Not necessarily to evade customs, just to be well out of the way!

Poor Ollie Burton had his camera on his lap, and they asked all about it. How long had he had it, was it new, are there other bits for

156

it... and as he could show no receipt to show that he had legally bought it they confiscated the lot! Bloody ridiculous, we all agreed. What did it matter if someone in the Forces, defending the West, happened to have a duty-free camera or a simple umbrella?

Filton had a big runway that had been extended, and they demolished a small village in doing so, for the huge Bristol Brabazon that never went into production. (The extension was needless, as it turned out, as with its eight engines the prototype plane took off in a surprisingly short distance.)

On one flight I was Number 4 to Boss Lambert. Normally we would split off into pairs to land, but this time on this large runway he told us all to stick with him and we landed as a finger four. I easily proved I could stick there with flaps, dive brakes and perfectly follow everything he did.

On one of those trips PG Smith, who as I said was an amazing pilot, went off on one ghastly day to do some instrument flying, and I was to follow him. I was extremely good at formation flying by this point and I followed him up into cloud at 300 feet and we were still in it at 30,000 feet. He was going all over the place, and I was convinced we were doing steep turns, rolls and loops, but as I was watching him intently to be able to follow close in the cloud I was not able to glance at my instruments to be sure. When we landed I asked PG, "What the hell did we do up there in the cloud?" He shrugged, taciturn as ever, "Nothing much." So I was never quite sure what happened!

We were doing very low pretend rocket attacks from our Vampires on the Army's tanks and vehicles. One day we were taken out to Salisbury Plain in a lorry to meet the troops. I spotted a Flight Lieutenant navigator who was there as an observer or something, and I recognised him as the instructor of my navigation course at Cottesmore. He had not been a natural teacher and was quite poor at explaining certain things, at least to me. Navigation was not an easy subject for me for some time. I found I had to ask quite a few questions to really grasp the detail of it, which I eventually did as I became quite expert. One day in the classroom, when I put my hand up again, he said "Oh, my little lamb, what is it now?" And after that he never stopped calling me "my little lamb". You bastard, I thought during the course, but had to put up with it. When I saw him that day, I glared very hard at him, and despite his poor teaching he could see from my Wings I had made it as a pilot.

We participated in Exercise Cirrus at Twente in Holland to intercept a flight of Avro Lincolns. It was a miserable wet and misty stay with damp beds in our tents.

Mike Scarrot in our tent.

Ground Crew producing hot water for a five-star wash room!

The fertile minds of our ground crew had invented a way of producing some warmish water and a washroom. They were a great group of lads but not always appreciated by some officers, sad to say.

We flew on from Twente to Soesterberg in Holland for Ex. Pinnacle, which was a series of dummy raids on London. One of these was the Staines raid, being a simulation of a 100-bomber attack on England, using Staines Reservoir as a target. Three Wings had to all form up in poor weather, being careful to avoid the big aerials sticking up at Hilversum, and then flew in a huge formation towards London at 30,000 feet.

I was number 57. For the whole trip the cockpit was icing up until it had got so bad that I could barely see the guys either side of me to formate on. I thought, this is getting a bit hairy and if the others are having the same trouble then there is a high chance of collisions.

We got there safely and we turned over Staines reservoir, being attacked by UK-based Meteors, going in and out of us, until the simulation was over. We turned back towards Germany and I looked at my fuel gauge. The Boss had said if you are below a certain figure when we depart from Staines, drop out and get refuelled at RAF Manston before you come back.

I said on the R/T I was dropping out for refuelling. I was actually very glad to get away from the formation as I was still a bit iced up. I had to get a homing, dropping down slowly over East Kent until eventually I could see my destination.

RAF Manston was an emergency return airfield with FIDO fog dispersal equipment and an extra wide emergency runway. The airstrip was on a slight hill and had a bit of a ramp like an aircraft carrier at the end. I could see a Lancaster was just landing.

I was getting very low on fuel so I came round from the west, the wrong way, as it should have been from the east with the current wind. I didn't know what channels they were on and had no idea if they were getting my messages or not. Just as I started to land a Meteor took off towards me, literally only twenty feet over my head. That was a bit hairy and exciting but that close encounter was never mentioned.

It turns out I knew the pilot of the Lancaster, Sid Aldridge, who had been on my course. He was just passing through from abroad and we had a bit of a chat. I refuelled and carried off back at low level all the way by myself, at 100 feet over the North Sea. I came to the coast of Holland, skimmed over the islands, over the greenhouses and in to Germany. Most enjoyable! I climbed up to get a homing back to RAF Celle and that was the end of an exhilarating trip.

I maybe was a bit fuel greedy the way I flew, as I was not aware of others who ran out of fuel that trip. Engines did differ a bit of course. Maybe my kite had not filled up as much as it should have been? I was often Number 4 in formation and that position did take the most throttle work to keep in position and hence use the most fuel. Number

1 uses the least as he simply shows the others the way he wants to go and doesn't have to do the constant engine adjustments. The fact is my gauge had been below the figure stipulated by the Boss so I did as I was told and refuelled.

That time at Manston was not my only unexpected brush with a Meteor. For a mass flypast of the Brussels Air Show in 1952 we flew to RAF Wildenrath to assemble and refuel and then we all lined up. Wildenrath was a new airfield that had just been built and there were piles of excavated red sand still standing around. When we took off as a bunch the sand got stirred up by the jet engines ahead and you couldn't see a bloody thing in front of you. It was just a case of hoping that no one had collided or belly landed in front. Once we had climbed out of the dust we could see everyone else and formate again.

There were a hundred of us ready to do a flypast over Brussels and we had to make a huge formation. Needless to say it is very dangerous with so many aeroplanes in the sky, especially as the weather was vile and visibility poor. We made this big formation and were heading off, quite nicely stepped down tightly, one behind the other, all in fours at slightly different heights. That was four lines of 25 fours. We will never see anything like it again these days.

Suddenly out of nowhere came two Meteors at great speed. Flying straight for us, they passed right through the middle of our formation. Golly, was that a momentary shock for us and no doubt for them too. It was incredibly lucky that they somehow missed us all at that speed and it all happened so quick that we didn't really have any time to worry about it!

We had an exercise in England, Ex. Flamingo, where we came over as a squadron to Wattisham to attack bombers and this was also the time we visited RAF Trimley Heath GCI Station.

There were no bombers based in Europe, only the UK, which is why we came over. For the exercise they assembled about fifty Super Fortresses flying in a box, like they did in the Pacific. We were going to attack them with Meteors from one side and Vampires from the other. Head on attacks are bloody dangerous. You were coming in from one side with your camera gun then suddenly you see a Meteor or two screaming in at you from the other side and that quite puts you off. Some of them were weaving through the bombers. Foolishly dangerous way to carry on, we thought; it should at least have been done in separate waves. I guess they wanted to try all sorts of scenarios as they did not know what the Russians might throw us: lots of bombers, lots of MiGs or both.

During 22 flights in various different kites on that exercise I had R/T failure eleven times and also blew two blades off a turbine. At one point the Chiefy was getting a bit fed up and asked if I was sabotaging my planes or something, and he was only half joking! Just bad luck, of course.

The lad pictured always helped me "swing the compasses" which had to be checked every so often for accuracy. There were two compasses, a Pilot's P-type compass and a Magnusson compass in the wing. Both had to be swung to check they were accurate. The Germans were very organised, as back at Gütersloh they had built in a turntable in the parking area, operated by a diesel engine, so you could swing the fighter around to calibrate accurately. Without a turntable at Celle we had to be manually oriented on the wheels which was much harder work.

Ground crew looking after our kites

162

16 Squadron Pilots in June 1952:

1. Richard "Greg" Gregory
2. Jean Paul (French Sergeant)
3. Ron Taylor – nice lad
4. Self (rear)
5. Bill Lacey
6. Ken Ashman
7. Aubrey C Covington
8. CO RUP de Burgh
9. Al Philips
10. Slim Holiday (rear)
11. Bysshe Shelley
12. Jerry Eades
13. Captain St Martin (French)
14. Mike Scarrot
15. Pete Gooding was a nice bloke.
16. Joe Greene who had Cody the dog.

Notes:

2 & 13. We had two French pilots on exchange posting to us, but I don't ever remember any of us going to a French squadron.

10. Slim was a bit of a twit at times! One day he was given the task of taking a Bishop, who had never flown before, up in a Meteor. Slim threw him all over the sky and made the poor old bugger sick. Daft, and he got told off for it.

12. Eades was the son of an Air Commodore who was the Commandant at RAF Cranwell. He thought he was a big cheese like his father so he was very aloof and pompous and did not get on with anyone. I don't know if he made it to Air Cdre like he wanted.

14. Mike was another son of an Air Commodore. Nice lad, absolutely super, but a bit scatty! He went off on a trip from Gütersloh to Twente and somehow got lost. He saw an airfield and landed on it. It was Wildenrath, just being built at the time, but luckily the runway was finished! He taxied over to some workmen and they pointed him the right way and he took off. Eventually he ran out of fuel and bailed out of his Meteor! There is a court of inquiry and lots of questions after a plane incident, especially when one was lost. He came back and told us about it. He was one of the boys and chatted like the rest of us.

163

Some pilot friends at Celle.
Behind: Nobby Clark.
Front: Dave Garrett, Whisky Walker, Bob Sowery (My best man),
Simmy Simpson and Jimmy James

I can't remember what airfield this was but too good a photo not to put in

Self on the Rifle Team

Chapter 22
Towing at Acklington until Demob

I was on my way home in October 1952, having done my two and a half years out in Germany, and made my way to the Air Ministry to get a new posting. What I didn't know was the police had been trying to catch up with me to tell me that my mother was very ill. When I was finished in London I went on to Mollie's house in Ipswich at which point the police did finally catch up with me. They knocked and asked if Sgt Pilot Rutherford was here, and by that time it was to inform me, "We are very sorry, but your mother has died." Obviously, I was very sad that I had not heard in time to get up to see her to say my goodbyes, but at least I was on leave and able to attend the funeral.

My last seven months in the service period that I had signed up for was a posting to RAF Acklington where I was towing gliders and flags as air gunnery targets.

Squadron pilots came there for target practice just as I used to do myself at Sylt. The system here was that I towed a big flag or sometimes an old glider behind a Meteor Mk 8 - and what a delightful aeroplane to fly! The flag was a big sheet of canvas that used to flap about like mad. It had a big bar to spread it, with a heavy weight on one end to keep it vertical, and from both ends of that bar two cables formed a triangle to join on to one towing cable which trailed about 100 feet behind my plane.

The routine was to take off at 160 knots, climb to 22,000 feet then join my tow line (the course). It was usually very boring, just flying a steady course up to Holy Island and back again until the target needed replacing. In the back of your mind, however, there was a constant dread of being hit with live 20mm cannon rounds if someone continued firing and got you in their sights!

Off shore were Russian trawlers covered in antennae. Every so often we flew over in a Meteor to look and see what they had got and to let them know we were watching them just like they were watching us. They could jangle our R/T transmission, making a deafening noise like a whole roomful of empty tin cans being shaken and banged together. On those days it was extremely tempting to give them a few rockets!

The pilots came to stay for a month and in that time did a lot of target shooting and plenty of practice in perfecting their curves of pursuit, firing and breaking away.

The cannon rounds in each attacking aircraft had different coloured paint on them that left a mark of paint around the hole so that these could be counted to give a score to each pilot back on the ground. (Of course, it was difficult to be entirely accurate with the counts if they happened to hit the same spot as another round had already passed through.)

One day someone flew so close that he hit the spreading bar and embedded it in his wing, but he was good enough to recover. I watched him practise his stalling to see how that worked with the damage and a chunk of extra metal on one side, and then he brought it down and landed safely. Next thing I heard was that he got court martialled and was kicked out. To me that was a mistake, as when you get that kind of experience it is good to be alive and able to share it with other people. He made a bad mistake for sure - no one else ever managed to hit the flag before, as far as I knew - but he recovered the situation and landed safely. He should have been kept on.

My wife Mollie was with me and we lived at Warkworth for those six months. We lodged with the Robinsons from Yorkshire in their Bed and Breakfast. The husband was the odd job man around the town, and he could fix anything with his bag of tools. The butcher down the High Street, Alfie Moore, was an old man and he said he knew my Dad and had done business with him at times.

166

I never got accommodation allowance for some reason, so the rent was out of my own pocket. Everyone had coal fires and Mollie complained that every time she put her washing out the soot came down and ruined her washing. That made her mad!

Another pilot was lodging in the High Street and we cycled together the four miles to camp and back. It was not far but it was very hilly and made for good exercise!

Warkworth is a lovely old town and I already knew there is no more beautiful English river than the Coquet, wending its way across Northumberland from the Cheviot Hills to the coast near Warkworth. We would often walk to the river and visit Warkworth Castle which was built in a loop of the river. The inventor William Armstrong, founder of Armstrong Whitworth (later Vickers Armstong), devised the world's first hydroelectric power scheme at his Cragside mansion on a tributary of the Coquet near Rothbury.

Warkworth Castle

In 1953 we also went on our first holiday together in England. Unfortunately, we chose Lowestoft where it drizzled every damn day!

We had had some nice breaks back in Europe. As well as at the beach at Scharbeutz, we went to Bad Harzburg in the Harz

Mountains (very close to the East German border) and to the Tyrol in Austria for skiing.

In January 1945 I had signed up for three years as an air gunner and during those three years they started training pilots again, at which time I signed up for another five years. After this point I left the RAF, on account of Mollie's wishes. She thought it would be a good idea to get out while I could, after I had already got away with a mid-air collision and three forced landings. She considered that was enough of my lives used up.

Whenever there was an air accident in Germany the telegram went straight to her desk for the AOC. She had seen my wheels-up Meteor accident report arrive on May 24th when we had only just met.

Worse, Mollie was visiting me one evening when I was in the Gütersloh hospital for some minor complaint. We saw some men carrying the coffin of someone from 93 or 94 Squadron. I asked one of them, "Who is this?"

"I didn't know him, but there was not much left. We needed bricks." They used to do that, put bricks in the coffin to make it feel like a body when there were only a few remains.

By sheer bad luck I learned that just after I left Germany, the NCO pilots on 16 Squadron who had longer to serve were all commissioned. I had missed that boat yet again and it became abundantly clear that a commission was *really* not part of my destiny!

I personally felt I should have stayed in the RAF. I could have gone for the full 22 years and surely one day would have been commissioned and eventually earn a decent pension!

However, the decision had been made and I left the Royal Air Force on June 2nd 1953, which was Coronation Day.

Mollie on a holiday walk
in Bad Harzburg

Chapter 23
Mollie's lot from Suffolk

M ollie's real name was Muriel Grace Grimwood, but she was never called Muriel and particularly so after she started out on her life's great love - playing the pianoforte at seven years old. There was a funny little popular song from before the First World War entitled *Mollie O'Morgan with her little organ* which helped her pet name to stick.

Mollie's parents were a nice couple, originally from the Stowmarket area, with whom I got on well.

Grace, Jack and Mollie

Her mother was Grace Emmeline Moore who had worked in the Woolwich Arms Factory during WW1 making shells.

A rough map of the East Anglian places coming up in my story

Her father, Josiah Isaac Grimwood but known as Jack, was a big, strong chap. Cheerful, although he could be the opposite when he wanted to, he was a Suffolk policeman with collar number 16 when I knew him, and I enjoyed hearing about his interesting background.

(The 1-6 combination came up a number of times in my life, I noticed. 361 ATC squadron, 61 bomber squadron, 16 fighter squadron and now Policeman 16, and there were others. The call sign allocated to me in Germany was Liner One-Nine. Don't know how or why that arose, but I know it should have been Liner One-Six!)

171

Jack's father, John, was involved in the malting of oats all around Stowmarket for one of the breweries. Oats and barley had to be taken up to the raised floor where it was toasted on big stones with holes in them. Jack helped his dad by carrying two hundredweight bags up the steps, where many people could barely carry one hundredweight.

John had a pony and trap and earned £5 a week back in the early 1900s and he had ready access to beer! If he wanted his garden dug for vegetables he would get a barrel from the brewery, set it up in the garden and tell the locals, "Come along, drink as much as you like, as long as we get all this turned over today!"

Jack started his working life as a chauffeur for a family in Anglesea Road, Ipswich so he was driving a long time before most people. He also had his own motorbike where not many people had one of those either. When he went off to fight in the Great War his younger brother took possession of the motorbike and crashed it for him.

When he joined the Army, and they found he could drive, he was sent to the Army's lorry depot at Kempton Park. He was taken out in a lorry with several others to have his driving test. When his turn came they had stopped on a hill and he clambered out of the back and climbed into the driver's seat.

The instructor said, "So, Grimwood. It says here you can drive?"

"Yes, Sir."

"Can you do a hill start?"

"Yes, Sir."

"Well off you go then."

So Jack put it into gear, moved forward ten yards up the hill, at which point the chap said, "Stop! Well done. You've passed."

After that he got paid 8s a day, which he said was more than a Lieutenant, just because he could drive. After doing heavy vehicle driving he somehow ended up driving for General Farquharson. Jack obviously made it through the war, unlike his brother Bertie who was killed on Hill 60 at Ypres in 1915.

After the Armistice was signed in 1918 Jack thought he was going home to see his sweetheart, but he wasn't. Instead, the General told him they were going to Cologne as their part in the Army of Occupation.

After arriving in Cologne the General said he had to go away to the War Office in London for a week or two. Jack thought, "What's good for the goose is good for the gander." He went to see the Regimental Sergeant Major and said, "Sir, as the General has gone off for ten days, can I have a few days leave for myself?" He was issued a leave chitty and went home.

Jack's sweetheart, Grace

While he was there he went to the Ipswich Police Station where Captain Arthur Schreiber, the Chief Constable, was desperately seeking new policemen. Jack met with him and said he wanted to join the police when he was finished as a driver in the Army.

"A driver, eh? Very good! You can start tomorrow."

"No, Sir, I have to go back to Germany and clear up my things."

"I'll take care of all that," said Schreiber. And so he did, as Jack never went back (and never saw any of his kit again) and he was never officially demobbed.

I teased him about that, saying, "You are a deserter, then. You are still officially in the Army!"

He laughed and replied, "Maybe I should go and collect my back pay!"

Chief Constable Schreiber took on Jack as his driver as there were not many from Suffolk who could drive in those days. Jack drove him all over the place for many years. His picture is in the Suffolk Police Museum as a driver of the buses during the 1926 General Strike, one of very few able to drive large vehicles. Then at some point Jack went on the beat.

He had the trick of getting into the shadows so he could see what was going on without anybody seeing he was there. One night he was on duty on the Felixstowe Road when he heard a peculiarly loud shuffling and wondered what the heck it was. Then a little Indian man walked past and the shuffling got louder and louder, until an elephant loomed out of the darkness! They were from a visiting circus.

When he was at the end of his beat in Belstead he had to wait near the brook until his inspector came to sign him off. For a joke, Jack would hide so the inspector couldn't initially find him and would think he was skiving off. One warm night he was standing in a big stone gateway with ornaments on it when he took his helmet off to mop his brow. Suddenly, out of the dark, a big black cat jumped off the wall onto his head and gave him the fright of his life.

In the town there was a prostitute, named Ellen ___, who was quite a nuisance when she got drunk. Jack was doing point duty in central Ipswich when someone called him over to a trolley bus to deal with a drunken woman. He went on board and found it was Ellen, arguing loudly with everyone. When she saw him in uniform, she leapt up on the hanging handles and hung up there. He ordered her to get down, whereupon she peed on him!

Jack was known to be able to pack a punch on Friday nights around the pubs in the dock area of Ipswich. Jack was 6'2 with fists like hams and if he hit you with one of those... One night there was a call from The Beehive pub in Upper Orwell street saying a sailor was in trouble with some soldiers and needed help. Jack got there and found these soldiers were trying to stuff the poor matelot down a drain. He waded in and banged them about until he had rescued the sailor, although a sleeve was torn off his tunic in the fight.

He retired from the police just after the Second World War. He wanted to complete the full national insurance contributions for his pension so he worked as a driver for Hewitts the grocer. As a side line he also did a lot of driving instruction.

174

Jack retained his strength and when he was 84 I saw him take a railway sleeper, turn it on its side, and in one day he had hand-sawn right down the middle. He used these pickled sleepers as planks to work on his garden. I caught that habit off him, using planks to make walkways in my own gardens.

Jack and Grace had purchased 426 Wherstead Road, Ipswich, a brick terraced house with a long garden where they brought up their three children who all went to Northgate High School.

Jack on his BSA with sidecar and his two sons aboard

The first son was Geoffrey who won lots of school prizes. During the war he joined the Army and was promoted to Major. He went to work for a company in Maidstone as a clever electrician who invented electric motors for different special requirements. He later became MD of Broadbents of Huddersfield. His son Clive who is now the Managing Director was, as it happens, doing research at Cambridge University when his cousin, our daughter, Lois was studying there and they were friendly. We didn't get on well with Geoffrey, though, and sadly that side of the family has not been in contact for years.

The second child was Jack, known as John to his friends, but as Ivan to the family! He was a good-looking lad and I always liked him, as he was good for a few funny tales. He joined the Royal Navy in June 1940 as a probationary writer and was on the minesweeper HMS *Fitzroy* when she hit a mine and sank in the

North Sea. He came home just in trousers and a string vest, being all he had left after losing everything when his ship went down!

After the war he became a Chief Petty Officer and then became commissioned with some senior appointments well worthy of their own telling, if it was not for the Official Secrets Act!

He was made Captain and, when stationed in the Far East, one weekend he took his wife to an uninhabited island with just the sand, sea and a few trees for company. Elisabeth asked John for a cigarette from her coat which lay on the sand. He reached in the pocket and felt something sharp: he had been

stung by a scorpion that had crawled inside. He felt more and more ill as time went on, but there was nothing they could do about it as they had to wait until the boat came back to pick them up before sunset. He was not right for months. If I had been with them, I'm afraid I would have said, "I told you smoking is bad for you!"

The third of Grace and Jack's children was of course my Mollie. As a little girl she had a suitcase that she carried everywhere. Her mother told me that this behaviour drove her batty!

Mollie always loved her music. She says, "My brothers said I had nothing up top, but I proved them wrong. I was very good at music where they weren't, so I would play a piece on my piano to shut them up. Both my parents loved music but did not play themselves."

Mollie has arthritis in her hands now, perhaps because she has worn out her fingers with so many years of typing and piano playing! She got to Grade VIII and the same lady who taught her began to teach me and got me up to Grade II. My family had not been at all musical, so it was a totally new experience for me. Mollie's piano teacher was very old by then who only taught our own children for a short while before she died.

Mollie's suitcase and playing with Dad's point duty gear

Mollie on parade

177

Mollie had been a WAAF for 5 years 75 days as a Clerk GD (General Duties). She was all set to be commissioned, as Earl Bandon was entitled to have a commissioned PA, but I came along to upset the applecart and spoil her career. She would have been an officer like her brothers, and that would have helped shut up their teasing!

I got to know some of Mollie's relatives and will mention a couple of them. Aunt (Violet) May was divorced from her husband called Cleghorn who was a one-eyed, one-armed driver. (Don't ask how or why, as I don't know.) Aunt May ran a café called The Ritz in Ipswich, part of the big cinema which is now demolished. Since May was always working, her son Geoffrey Cleghorn spent a lot of time with his Aunt Grace. That was why we saw so much of him and became very fond of him.

Geoffrey went to Ipswich Art School and moved to London where he knew many people in the top pop groups of the 1960s like the Rolling Stones, The Who and the original Pink Floyd with Syd Barrett. He went off in their buses on various tours. He never played any sort of instrument as far as we know, he just liked hanging around with them. He was involved in painting up the tour bus for Paul McCartney's Wings tour in 1972.

He had a nice Lambretta scooter all polished up with plenty of chrome, until he crashed it, and then it got pinched. He wore a fine pair of blue or yellow leather boots his mother bought for him. I think

A picture Geoffrey sent to Mollie

he had a whale of a time in the Swinging Sixties! He was a bit of a wanderer and I don't know what happened to him.

Mollie's Aunt Doris had two boys, Roy and Ian Macdonald. Roy joined the Army and was killed and buried out in Korea when he was just a young man. I used to lay a wreath on behalf of the Air Crew Association at Christchurch Park on Remembrance Sunday. I was talking to a chap from the Suffolk regiment who, it turned out, had carried Roy's body back from where he was killed.

The younger son Ian was doing very well at school when I came home on leave to marry

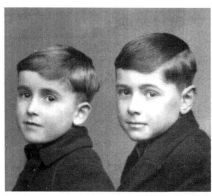

Mollie. We visited that family and he asked me about the RAF. Lo and behold, he joined the RAF himself and got into Cranwell where I heard he won the sword of honour and the aerobatic prize. He went on to fly Canberras, which he liked, and then Vulcans which he didn't, as he said it was just a flying computer. We lost contact but I heard he became a clergyman.

A happy picture of Grace and Jack

179

Chapter 24
Lois, Max and Crumpy

We lived with Mollie's parents for a while until we got our first house at 35 Preston Drive on the newly built Castle Hill housing estate in Ipswich. We bought it brand new for £1,580 and moved in on 31st of January 1956.

I don't remember the exact numbers but when I left the RAF I received a lump sum gratuity of about £400 for my time as a pilot plus £75 due for my service as an air gunner. What was peculiar was that £14-11s had been deducted for "barrack damages at Lytham St Anne's", a place I had never been to! I really should have followed that up as I expect it was a ruse and went straight in somebody's pocket. I had also received the legacy my father had left, which amounted to £425 over the 18 years it had been held in readiness for me by my half-brother Tom. All that money was very handy for setting up home. We were able to put down a deposit on the house and spend £240 on G-plan furniture (and we still have some of that!)

There was a heavy snowfall when we moved in and I was afraid the pipes might freeze, so I went up into the loft to have a look. I had paid extra for cladding and found this had not been done so I stuffed old socks and towels around the pipework. I went to complain to the builder. He said that he had done it, but then stopped and said, "Number 35? Oh hell, I did the one next door by mistake!" He rectified that in due course. The neighbour who had got the free lagging was a paint salesman. We got off to a bad start as he seemed a horrible bloke until we thawed out (ha ha!) and became friends.

There was mud everywhere when we first moved in but over the years I created a lawn and garden with some very welcome help from my father-in-law.

Old Jack the Gardener

180

We lived there for fifteen years and both our children were brought up there; Lois who arrived in the maternity hospital in 1956 and Max at home with lady Doctor Healey's help in 1960. He was a big baby and poor Mollie was in labour for 38 hours!

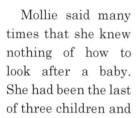

Mollie said many times that she knew nothing of how to look after a baby. She had been the last of three children and never had to tend to a younger sibling. She looked to the local NHS clinic for guidance. She had enjoyed her secretarial career and time in the WAAF and it came a bit of a shock to come back to be a mother and housewife. She never liked cooking and hence was not terribly good at it. (Mind you, I can't cook either: sausages or a fried egg, if I'm lucky.)

Once Mollie's new teaching career was underway the running of the household was more or less handed over to the teenage Lois. Lois says:

"Money was always scarce. It was very much a pay cheque to pay cheque lifestyle whilst Dad was the only bread winner. Waste was not allowed, especially food. Fortunately, Dad had a strong constitution and rarely got sick from insisting on using food past its

decent life or from clearing up food from his children's plates! Dad could frequently be heard to say, 'There are starving children in Biafra and you are leaving that fat off the meat?' Mum dismissed these outbursts as the result of a deprived childhood, which in retrospect was probably on the mark. In later years, when I was making the meals, I arranged the dishes strategically to make very sure that there was not going to be an issue of waste for anyone!

"Apart from trips to the Suffolk coast on summer weekends, the household seemed to be one of permanent work. Dad had one project after another to pursue: house painting, installing gas central heating, and then taking up an Open University degree on top of his teaching jobs. He would take bags of school books to the beach for marking, intending to work, but then he'd give in to the sun and sea."

Our children went to the newly built local school, Castle Hill Infants and Primary School, and they both went on to Northgate School, like their mother had before them.

Mollie had taken up smoking during her time in the Forces but in the early 1960s she gave it up. There was not enough income for her to continue her habit and I am sure my nagging must have helped to get her off it!

In the early 1970s we moved to 49 Westbury Road to be nearer to the school. Lois was cycling home in the dark and she had to stop in the middle of the bypass to turn right and we were worried that she might be knocked off, as the lights from her bike dynamo did not work when she was stationary and waiting to turn.

At that time Max was about ten years old and he played with some American children down the road. They were looking after a little Yorkshire terrier for an American from the US Bentwaters Air Base who had parted company from his wife. She had gone back to the States and he could not look after the dog on his own with his work commitments. Max often played with this little dog  and fell in love with it, and he kept telling us about how much he wanted it and that it was up for sale.

Mollie told me to go and tell the people we could not have a dog and that was final. I was just putting central heating in our house, and all the money I had left in the bank was £15. I went to see these people and they said, "But it has to be sold!" How much did they want for it? Naturally, it was fifteen pounds. I said, "I'll take it!" And it was the best £15 pounds I ever spent.

For sixteen years we kept that lovely dog of various names. Her pedigree name was Crumpet of Brentwood, but following the Carry On films and such like, we could hardly go about calling out "Crumpet"! Lois called her Crumpy, Max named her Crum or Crumb (as she was not big enough to be a full slice) and Mollie's favourite term was, "Come on,  chuchuface!" The new pet responded to all her names with glee and was taken for multiple walks each day and, despite her tiny size, kept up with all her tall owners for many years.

After five years we moved to 337 Main Road, Martlesham. Lois liked the look of it in an estate agents' window. She said, "Dad, we should buy his lovely house!" But it was £20,250. I said, "We can't afford that, this one is only worth about £11,000!" But after a while we did go to look at it and Mollie and I fell in love with it too, so that's where we went. With Mollie earning as well by now we could meet the mortgage rates.

Lois went on a week's art holiday with a group to Spain in her late teens having raised the money with a summer job making interior pieces for stereo equipment. She spent a week on the south side of the Pyrenees. A lady with her group made a lovely painting of Lois but she was asking £50 pounds for it and we simply didn't have it. She took a photograph of it for Lois to keep and Lois kept her address. Some while later  I had the money together and phoned the lady up and asked if I could buy it, but she said, "Oh no, I have painted over that long ago.". That was a great shame as it was a lovely picture.

Both of our children worked very hard and did well for themselves. Lois read history at Girton College, Cambridge where she earned a

First, and then went up to Oxford when she earned another! She married a reader at Cambridge, Robert Scribner, and then they moved to the USA when he was appointed Professor at Harvard. They gave us two lovely grandchildren, Nell and Sam who have both qualified as psychologists. Bob sadly died and Lois remarried to Howard (Howie) Moffett.

Nell and Sam

I got on well with the Principal of the Ipswich Art School on St George's street. He said to me, "There is no future in commercial art, or graphics, so don't let your son choose that." But that's exactly what Max did! He did graphic art at the Middlesex Polytechnic and has made a very good living out of it and is now a marketing and technical consultant for various US and UK payment specialists. He married Alex and we have two more lovely grandchildren, Ben who is in IT and Katy who is at equine college.

Max on his motorbike

Ben and Katy

184

Chapter 25
Mother, Sep and my half-siblings

Mother in 1950

Mother, Ethel Alice, was born in Seghill, Northumberland on June 21st 1900. That was the same year as the Queen Mother was born, but she only did half as well in years. She died aged 52 but I am not sure why. (I never got to see her death certificate because I was repatriating from Germany when she died and my siblings dealt with all matters.)

I wondered if my Mother died so young from too much smoking? With my passion against it, I certainly assumed it had adversely affected her lungs and heart.

I never liked smoking. Nobody smoked cigarettes back on the farm but Pop Finlay soon got my mother started on "tabs". They would buy five Woodbines for tuppence and each smoke at least ten a day. I tried tabs at school, as we all did, but didn't get on at all with smoking and didn't persevere. I don't know which of my friend's daft idea it was to buy cinnamon sticks from the Chemist and try smoking them at the old quarry! That was a dead loss as they weren't made for burning.

For years I have been like a broken record lecturing against smoking: "It will get you if you don't give it up!" My dear sister Ella married a heavy smoker called Mike Nolan, a foreman at International Paints in Gateshead making paint for ships. He got Ella a job testing paints in the laboratory. They both earned good money and seemed to spend most of it on tabs! When I had left home in Felling I was glad to leave all the smoke behind, but I had to put up with it every time I went to visit Ella and Michael and I kept asking them to stop.

Mike said, "I can give up any time."

"Really? Well how about now?"

"Oh no, I am not ready yet."

It turns out Mike never was quite ready and died of lung cancer. So did Ella, having given up but going back to it a few times. She was still happy and chirpy to the end, a lovable sister who I miss terribly. Ella had done a lot in running the household when our mother was ill and she never made a fuss.

During the war years I bought a Boots 6d diary, with a whole page for each day, in which I laboriously recorded a detailed historical record of the war, right up until 1944 when I left home for the Air Force. I shared a room with my brother Septimus. We had just one cupboard in our room, and I admit it was pretty much full of my stuff! Aircraft recognition books I had bought, the piece of a crashed aircraft that I had pilfered, shrapnel, models I had made, all my diaries and much more besides. Sep and I didn't think much of Pop at all, but he fought with distinction in the Second World War. He was cut out to be a good soldier, we felt. He had a wonderful set of medals, including a military medal, a MID, and with the maple leaf on the Italian Star medal ribbon this probably made quite a rare set.

When I asked Ella what had happened to the medals, she said our mother had thrown them all out. I said. "No! What else has she thrown away?" The answer was everything. All my diaries and belongings, and even my bicycle. I suppose my mother suspected I would never come back, and she cleared the cupboard out to give Sep more space. To hear that I had lost the lot was annoying, to say the least, but I still loved her.

I was close to Sep and we always got on well and would visit each other. As Mollie says, "Septimus had carrot ginger hair and a very thick North Country accent. Time and again I had to ask, 'Ralph what did he say to me?' I really didn't have a clue what he was saying in the early days!"

Sep worked for the National Coal Board (NCB) as a check weigh-man on the coal railway. He had a cabin on the south side of the River Tyne, at the colliery end, where he had to weigh wagons full of coal. There was a big chain, driven by a stationary engine, and on each end were attached a number of wagons. At his end these were filled with coal and then the chain dragged them down to the staithes to be emptied, meanwhile pulling all the empties back up to be refilled again.

Sep and Ella

Sep was a keen golfer and in 1953 he went to Austria on holiday with some friends from Tyneside where he met Mavis, who was chaperoned by her mother. They got on very well and arranged to go on holiday together to Norway... and her mother was there, again! Mavis said later, "My mother obviously did not trust her own daughter to behave herself!"

Sep promised he would regularly come down from Newcastle to see her in Berkhamsted, Hertfordshire. It was a lot of travelling, and he could not manage to visit often enough, so he wondered if he could get a job more locally. He went to the National Coal Board HQ and asked if they had any jobs down her way, and they said he could start right away. He went back home to give in his notice and collect his gear.

He had no qualifications to his name, yet he secured a very good job in coal sales and he thrived. He sailed up the ladder, becoming their number two man in sales. He knew everything about every sort of coals, where you found them, what they were good for, what they cost. He and Mavis were able to get married and settled down there, living in various places around Beds, Herts and Essex.

Mavis and Sep

Sep and I remained great friends all through life. Like me he had joined and loved the ATC and knew a lot about flying. He was too young for the war but became a civilian glider pilot and spent many happy hours at the London Gliding Club in Dunstable.

187

Sep's right eye was useless for some reason, since boyhood. They tried glasses to help but it never came right. Despite this he achieved over 100 hours on gliders. I took him up in an aerobatic plane I used at Ipswich Airfield, but Sep was not at all keen on the way I threw him around!

The final family member to mention was youngest brother John, the son of Ethel and John Finlay. I never really knew him as he was an infant when I left home. He cried like hell at mother's funeral in 1953, as he was only 13.

When he was older he drank and smoked too much and was a bit of a waster like his father. He had no qualifications from school but when he joined the army he did well enough to become a Sergeant on transport in Germany, again very much like his Da. As far as I know he never married before he died at a relatively young age, down in London.

Two farmers: Brother Charles and nephew George (the son of brother Tom) pictured in recent years

Swans on the River Coquet

188

Chapter 26
Teacher Training

So what on Earth was I going to do for my new career? I was in a dilemma and had no idea. I could not really go farming back in Northumberland with my half-brothers. I considered forestry and other things until I thought of teaching geography as I always loved maps and was very well read in all aspects of weather patterns.

As we discussed it together, Grace and Jack said to me, "You would certainly have to go to college. You still don't even speak English properly!" (In the mid-1950s Mollie's mother was still regularly heard to say, "What did he say?" even with my improving accent.)

ANY ADDITIONAL INFORMATION AND TYPE OF EMPLOYMENT FOR WHICH RECOMMENDED :—

Sgt. Pilot Rutherford has at all times been found to be a cooperative man in all that he has been asked to do. He has served overseas on a flying operation and in the U.K. Recently he has been employed on target towing duties while awaiting demob. This man has been proved to be keen, trustworthy, and efficient during his service, and his recommended to any employer who may want to employ him.

P. G. CAMEON (Signature of Commanding Officer)
(NAME IN BLOCK LETTERS)
Rank *FLT. LT.* Date *30.3.53*

H.Q. A.R.S.
30 MAR 1953
R.A.F. ACKLINGTON

I went to the Education Office in Ipswich to see the Education Chief. Mollie had known his son who had been an air gunner but was shot down and killed. She told me the chief was a nice chap, which he certainly was and he helped me to apply to training college.

I chose geography as my main subject with physical education as my secondary subject, and arts and crafts as the third. The best college to do that combination turned out to be Shoreditch Training College (STC), formerly of London but recently relocated to Englefield Green, near Windsor in Surrey.

When I got to Shoreditch I was interviewed by the deputy, a very nice gentleman called Mr. Charles who was married to a French woman. He threw in a lot of French words and expressions all the time and I didn't speak any of that! He said the staff were all interested in having an ex-jet pilot join their course, as they had never had one before. He interviewed me and showed me how to write a good letter of application, as my written English was pretty poor. I sent that in and had a second interview with someone from London University which resulted in me being offered a place from September 1953 on a two-year course.

I was asked to write an article for the college magazine about a typical sortie in Germany, from beginning to end. This caused some unexpected problems! There were a small number of trainees who were Communists and they got very agitated that one of their peers had been prepared to fight against their comrades. There was an ex-Navy chap called Alan Stamper from Nottingham on our course but as he didn't stick his head up like I had done they left him alone.

One of these Commies asked me, "Would you have dropped a bomb on Russia?"

"Yes, of course I would!"

That really got their goat and they came after me for a while. "Do you realise you kill people when you do that kind of thing?" Yes, yes of course I do. Damned cheek.

There was one chap called John and another big chap. They both came from Orpington, so for many years after that I was assuming that town in Kent must be a hotbed of communists! They were deadly serious about being anti-services and negative about everything to do with the Forces. I got fed up with them and let them know

In our accommodation hut. Spot the Communist!

very plainly that if they annoyed me any further I would biff them in the eye. They finally left me alone.

That reminds me. Next door to us in an upstairs flat at Felling was a chap called Robinson who went off to Spain to fight for the communist side against Franco and came home wounded. I used to talk to his son who seemed perfectly normal, unlike his Dad.

Communists aside, I enjoyed the course and made some good friends including my room mate Charlie Stobbs from Wales, Tim Yeo from Cornwall, and Henry Richards who was a skilful cabinet maker, also from Cornwall. Henry was in the next room to me and he taught me how to use woodworking tools as I had absolutely no idea how to use chisels or wood planes, prior to that.

I became Social Secretary and helped organise dances and other activities. I had a fairly decent singing voice and a nice little chap known as Happy Holliday took us for singing. He roped enough of us in for a small choir to sing Stainer's Crucifixion at the local church one Easter and that came out very well, we were told.

There were two clever lads who drew some magnificent coloured chalk pictures for every social event held in the Great Hall. These were done on a double-size black board and were a joy to behold.

Everyone had to do some PE, but some of us took it to a much higher level and hence we were called the muscle men!

About twenty of us went to stay at Bisham Abbey for a week's course in special sports. This very old-fashioned Bishop's residence was a fascinating old house with sweeping wooden staircases.

One of the events included canoeing on the Thames which happened to be in full flood. We were trying the slalom course, zig-zagging across the river between two sticks, when I caught the paddle on one of the sticks and dropped it from my hand. So there I was, shooting down the river without a paddle. Fortunately there were people swimming in the Thames, and someone was quick enough to retrieve my paddle and hand it back to me. Others further downstream were waiting to catch any people, paddles and canoes that got away! It was a very exhilarating week.

Our chief of PE was an ex-Olympic hurdler who also took us for technical drawing. As I played in the rugby team that he coached, I always found I was given 'A' grades for my rather average drawings!

With my height I played 2nd row lock, and my ears got so mashed up in the scrum I needed to buy a headcap. At one point my cauliflower ear got so bad I had to go to Windsor Hospital for a nurse to lance it to release the blood. I was amazed as she stuffed a whole metre of bandage into the flesh of my ear to soak it up! A week later she pulled it all out again, which was very painful indeed, and put a pad over my ear and stuck it down with plasters for a week until the wound healed enough to be exposed. I gained a few other injuries including a broken left middle finger and dislocated left shoulder.

A story went around that some years before, when playing a Roman Catholic college called St Mary's (known as "Simmaries"), that when the Shoreditch hooker crashed heads with their hooker he broke his neck and that killed him. We played them and they were indeed a dirty team. No broken necks that day, but it was a terrible match and they won as they always did. They didn't play for sport, they only played to win, by hook or by crook. I took a fist in the face once, but I am not sure now if that happened when we were playing them or not.

192

Things certainly did happen on the pitch! When we watched rugby together, Mollie often asked, "Are they allowed to do that?" Oh yes, I would reply.

One of my rugby pals was Garfield Owen from Newport RFC who played a few games as fullback for Wales. As social secretary I bought myself a penguin suit for the events. When Garfield went with Wales to Paris, where they won I think, he borrowed my evening dress suit to wear for the post-match dinner.

I didn't get home much during term time, but Mollie would come and see me at rare times and we'd stay at an hotel in Windsor. She brought her mother once, I think for the valedictory dance at the end of the course. I took them for a walk in Windsor Great Park when we came to a ditch. I tried to carry Grace over it but stumbled and manged to fall in it with her! Luckily the ditch was dry of water, but it was still rather an awkward moment.

Monkey puzzle tree in front of the college buildings

As part of the course we did teaching practice in schools to get the feel for being in a class. Henry and I were sent to Kingston Grammar for two weeks. When we got there that first morning, we arrived early on the bus before most of the teaching staff. In the staff room we found there were two big easy chairs by the fire and we sat there to wait.

The chair I parked myself in was the usual seat of a nasty Welshman. He didn't say anything at the time, but later that week I was allocated to him to do an English class with a sixth form group. He said, "I want you to do some past and present tense clauses with these boys." To be honest I had no idea what he was talking about. I wasn't even studying English. I stood there flummoxed and had to ask him to show me what he wanted, which he did. The sixth form quickly cottoned on to the fact I was a trainee, and they were laughing at me, but I had been in the RAF for nine years and it was like water

193

off a duck's back. I did wonder why a senior teacher would want to put a new student on the spot like that? Then it all became clear. Word had got around school of this trainee not being able to do what he was asked to do, so a more friendly teacher came up to me and said, "You know why this has happened? Well, you sat in his chair by the fire. You shouldn't have sat there."

"How on earth was I to know?"

"You weren't," he shrugged.

At the same school I was allocated to a handicraft teacher who was extremely helpful. He showed me how to do technical drawings on the board. He said, "Whatever you do, don't teach craft." And just as we were talking, I could see why. A member of staff came in with a broken chair. "Another one for you. Can you fix this for tomorrow?" and off he went again.

"You see what happens? They expect me to be their odd job man!"

So I never did teach that, even though I had been trained in metalwork, woodwork and book binding. We had to buy a cheap second-hand book, tear the cover off, and bind it back on. I bought one on sailing. When I had covered it in a special bookbinding cover I decorated the front with a sailing boat using coloured inks and gave that to my doctor, who was a sailor.

Henry and I went into Kingston one lunchtime where we walked past an antique shop. We saw in the window a rectangular brick-shaped copper bowl with little curly legs. It was planished, bent over the edge and had curved feet soldered on. It had a notable price tag on it. I said, "Henry! If we got some copper sheeting, you and I could make some of those and sell them to the antique shop!"

Every night we were working on crafts, unless there was a dance or something on. They were very long days. We bought some copper sheeting and started on this project one evening. We were working on the first one when the metalwork tutor came in and saw it. He said, "You are not to do that sort of thing for yourselves," and he made us stop and scuppered our get-rich-quick scheme. No time was your own time at college.

I remember making a sugar basin and a milk jug out of gilding metal. It was very difficult to get the spout right. It was supposed to be silver soldered on with a very close fit. It took me ages to get a spout fitted at all, and when I did it looked ridiculous. I was going to have them silvered but instead I stuffed them in the back of a cupboard and never looked at them again.

The people who went on to do a third year spent much more time on craft work and they would have all these things up for sale. When we finished at STC a whole group of us from East Anglia arranged a lorry to pick us all up and all our stuff, including craft work we had made, and do a round to deliver us all to our homes.

The new Air Forces Memorial was right next door to the college grounds. On the day that was opened by our new Queen a few of us went to watch. Richard Dimbleby was  there with his cameras and caravan for a BBC outside broadcast. He saw us sitting on the wall, to enjoy a grandstand view, so he came over and said, "Get off there, would you, and go away. I am trying to do a broadcast here." We told him where to go in no uncertain terms! We watched the whole proceedings and I felt proud to be there for my lost friends.

We had a few japes, as all students do. At the end of term we put the tutor's cars up for sale; this one was a bargain at only ten Woodbine cigarettes.

Me pretending to be a Roman athlete at Motspur Park

At the end of term in July the tutor in charge of rural studies at the college asked for volunteers to take various animals back home with them, to look after, and bring back after the summer holiday. I took Joey the rabbit home and Mollie's father got an old crate and modified it for him. We fed him rather too well and he became a very big rabbit. Too big to go back, and the chap had decided he wanted new stock anyway. We decided we should eat him! What a daft idea that was. First of all, nobody could kill him. So we got a butcher to come in to do that and skin him, then Grace cooked him

and we all looked at our plates and nobody could eat him, after all.

The course and full board was all paid for by the Government, and we only had to pay for supplies, paper and pens and so on, and any special additional courses we chose to do.

A chap from Goldsmiths College was running courses showing how to work cinematic cameras. I did all three levels from beginners to intermediate and advanced, as I recognised that films would probably be used increasingly in education and I was quite right.

One chap taught italic handwriting, using two pencils tied together to get a nice effect. We each paid £3 to him, about 100 of us, so he made £300 for a weekend's work! He had published a book on it that looked so splendid in its presentation that I really wanted to learn it. I later even bought an italic fountain pen with a broad nib and wrote like that for years.

I needed some of my own money for these extra courses and things and a few treats. We didn't have a lot of spare time but we sometimes found some weekend work to bring in some funds. Two of us went along to Express Dairies Nurseries several times. It was a long walk to get down there and hard grind.

We were potting young chrysanthemums or daffodil bulbs for 3s 6d an hour in which time we had to finish at least eight bowls.

Two of us went to Wentworth Golf Course to do caddying. I got paid five quid to carry this heavy bag three or four miles around the course, and help find the right clubs, and all that made it hard-earned money. As I had to walk there and back as well I was quite exhausted and only went the once, even though it was good money.

Mollie was very good and sent me a few bob every week. She had got herself a job whilst I was away, working for Fram Egg Producers, the big egg packers in Ipswich. She lived two miles away and would get a bus up to the Bell Inn and then walk to work.

She enjoyed her work as secretary for the MD, Mr. Frost, and his Deputy MD, and she organised them both very well. Mr. Frost got Mollie to modify the pension rules so that his pension would be guaranteed at an age below that which was normal. However, he didn't suffer good health and died before he got to that age anyway.

Mollie also checked in the men who collected the eggs around the area to record what they had brought in from where. Drivers would pick up eggs from all around the countryside and each farmer was given a blue chitty. I worked there for a couple of weeks myself and one of my jobs was to check these chits so we knew what each collector had brought in so he could be paid his dues.

Every single egg was held in front of a light, and if it glowed in a certain way it was rejected. That became a high-speed job and there were quite a few people working there examining all the eggs. The farmer would not get paid for those that were no good. They would phone up to complain, "There is nothing wrong with my eggs!" but of course at times they would pick them up from hedgerows and haystacks where they could have been sitting for quite some time before they were spotted and were no longer fresh.

Chapter 27
A teaching career

When college ended in July 1955 I came back for the August holiday and went straight to the Ipswich Education Office to ask how I went about getting assigned to a school. The friendly Chief introduced me to a lady (who later ended up as our next door neighbour in Martlesham, as it happened.) She arranged for me to visit some schools to see whether I liked them.

The first was Westbourne Secondary Modern. As the headmaster showed me round the departments we saw some chap go walking across the playing field with some boys. He shouted, "Where are you going." Something was shouted back, but he yelled, "Take them back at once!"

Back in his office he asked me to take a seat for a moment as he had one of the staff to see. The man came in, a big tall chap in glasses, and he had him in tears in minutes, tearing off a strip so rudely in front of me. I decided he must be a bully and that place was not for me. When I reported back that I didn't think much of his methods, they agreed he was a bit hard on staff.

Ralph Rutherford, qualified teacher

Next one to try was Tower Ramparts (which is no longer there in Ipswich, it's now a shopping arcade and bus station). I went to see Mr. George Heath and found he was a gentleman. "I see you did sport, and took PE special, and craft too!" I said yes but didn't want to teach craft (bearing in mind the advice I had been given.)

"Oh, that's a pity. Never mind." He showed me round the very old school to meet some staff and he offered me a job. I quickly worked out it would suit me well: it was close to the centre and near Mollie's parent's house, where we were staying, so I could cycle in. I went back to the Education Office and said I would like that job.

I got landed with a class of 12-year olds. In those days we were general teachers who could carry out a wide range of skills. As Mr. Heath knew I was keen on PE he asked me to take charge of the intermediate football team. On Wednesday afternoons I would take small groups of boys up to the field to trial them and gradually assembled a team for the Under-13s.

Then he said, "Now that you have a team, I am entering them for the football shield competition. We have never won it, but I really want us to!" Oh no, I thought, that's a very tall order! I certainly can't guarantee a win.

I developed a technique with the two wingers who were both nice lads (one became a sergeant in the Met. Police). I said for him to bring it wide down his wing, cross it over to the other winger, and he will then run in to take a shot on goal. And then you will do the same the other way around, so they don't expect it. It worked and we won the shield! George Heath was really chuffed and came to thank me very sincerely.

Some time after this I was ordered to go to a meeting of teachers which I came to realise was a National Union of Teachers (NUT) meeting. I had been enrolled into that by somebody when I was on teaching practice without realising the full import of what this would mean: I had to do what this union said.

I went along and at some point in the meeting, a chap at the front stood up and said, "I am Bob Cootes, the football secretary. I understand there is a Spitfire pilot here, called Rutterford, who wants to take over from me?"

I thought, they must mean me, but what is he talking about?

Someone else said, "Is Mr. Rutterford here? Would he like to put his hand up?" I did so, and the chap carried on, "All those in favour?" and lots of hand went up. He turned to me and said. "You are duly elected as Schoolboy Football Secretary." I had not even raised a word and they didn't even know my correct surname! The deputy head had clearly set me up for this and for six years I worked as secretary.

I did two years teaching at Tower Ramparts, and that went well, but then I wanted to try something different. I got a position at a primary school called Luther Road School (now Hillside Primary) which is where Mollie had gone as a girl.

I didn't have a watch at that time but Mollie had one that I had bought her as a present. I borrowed Mollie's watch for use at school. I was refereeing a football match and didn't realise the watch had come off my wrist on the pitch. I hadn't realised it was gone until the headmistress, Miss Hack, came in and asked if anyone had lost a watch. I looked down to see my bare wrist and described the watch which she then handed over. It looked muddy and knocked about, as if several people had stood on it, but I cleaned it up and gave it back to Mollie. She was not overly impressed but she still has it and it still works. I then decided I had better buy my own!

When I was a boy I had desperately wanted a watch and my parents bought me an Ingersoll pocket watch for 5s with a two year guarantee. This particular one went for two years and then it stopped. I decided to mend it. I took the back off and started undoing the works. When Mam saw me she said, "You can't do that, you will wreck it!" I took it all to bits and that was how it stayed. They got me another and that did the same, stopping not long after two years was up. That was the end of watches for me, for years, as I never got the ones I was promised from Grandad.

At Jet School we were issued an Omega pilot's watch. I came down one day from a high-altitude trip and took my two pairs of gloves off. I wore silk underneath and a chamois pair over the top of them. I found the glass had come off my watch which meant the hands had got bent and were sticking up all skew-whiff.

My instructor told me to go to the stores and see if they would replace it. A few months later, when the glass of the new one came off on another a high-altitude trip, I suddenly realised what was happening. The stores officer wondered, "What are you doing with my bloody watches?" and I told him the different coefficients of expansion for the plastic front and the metal body caused the metal to shrink more in the cold and squashed out the plastic. I had to make sure, from then onwards, that the watch kept covered inside my gloves and sleeve all the time when I was not consulting it. (We had no timepiece on our instrument panels.)

I lasted only one year in that school with Miss Hack, who was a very tough old bird. Every morning I heard her having a terrible go at Miss Bright, in the next classroom, until the poor girl was in tears.

200

I wondered why she was being so harsh, as that behaviour surely won't get the best out of any teacher.

One day Miss Hack came and stood outside my classroom, where I was teaching the kids to do writing in italics. She opened the door to march in and announce, "You are to stop doing that at once, Mr. Rutherford! We do the Marion Richardson system here."

I said. "I haven't got a clue what that system is, but I know this italics style and I like it, so I am teaching the children and they are doing very nicely."

"You are to stop it at once. Find out about Marion Richardson."

I was hopping mad with her. I asked Miss Bright what this style was and she showed it to me, just perfectly normal handwriting. "Oh, is that all it is?" But I found I couldn't do that style very neatly so I carried on with my italics.

Miss Hack got her own back on me. She said, "I want you to put a pantomime on for Christmas."

"I am sorry, you had better ask one of the other teachers. I have no clue how to do that."

"It is up to you to find out," she said with great delight, and off she marched.

As time went on two of the female teachers gradually took it off my shoulders and for good reason! I quietly withdrew from the project, putting very little into it, and just had to make sure the scenery stayed upright! We needed a stage and scenery and Miss Hack told me there are some bits of wood in the basement. She was right, they were only bits. Just scrap with only one decent sheet of hardboard.

We did Jack and the beanstalk, with no tree of course, so one of the ladies painted a beanstalk on the sheet turned sideways and the child had to pretend to climb in front of it.

Miss Hack got her claws into everyone as that was her personality. One day she was scuttling along in the corridor to the staffroom when she slipped and broke her arm. Everyone was secretly cheering that event, sorry to say. Three months later she slipped again and broke the same arm. I did think, "Serves her right, the miserable old devil."

Another thing she said to me was, "You have been trained in craft. I want you to get some materials from a hardware shop, offcuts of wood or anything that is going to waste, and then get the children to do some project using your tools."

"My tools?" I thought, "I value my tools more than that!" But I brought them in to school. Each day I collected an armful of offcuts from Browns the timber merchant until I had enough for everyone.

I had an idea for a project which was to make a tray for half-a-dozen eggs. It seemed simple enough: a piece of hardboard with holes in and two pieces of wood at the sides to raise it up. Cutting the six holes in hardboard without a proper vice was hard work as the brace drill kept springing out. For the whole year we soldiered on making bloody egg trays! Miss Hack liked them, but I was beginning to think I needed to get away from here or I will keep getting lumbered with more craft work without any proper equipment.

I went to the Education Office and asked if they had any more vacancies, and they needed a geography teacher at the brand new Thurleston School. I told Miss Hack I was leaving and she was very upset about it. She said, "You will be much better off here." I later realised she was right. If I'd had any sense I would have stayed there, as I might have got a headship fairly smartly once she had retired. (You needed to have a degree to become a Headmaster in Secondary School by this time.)

I'll give her one due. She had an annual test that she personally concocted for the two top classes. The test covered English, arithmetic, history and geography. She would mark them to her standard and then parcelled them up to put in her cupboard.

After she had retired a chap called Stan Frost became the Head, and I bumped into him several times with school sport commitments. One day he said to me, "You used to teach at Luther Road under Miss Hack?" I agreed, and told him she was a tough nut, always finding trouble.

"Do you remember her cupboard where she stored the exam results? They went back 30 years and it took us ages to clear it out. It was a very good test. The children didn't get given a certificate though, so we assume it was just for her own satisfaction."

Miss Hack got very ill in a nursing home where one of Mollie's aunts, Doris, happened to be working. Doris came to me and asked,

"Will you please come and visit Miss Hack? She is on her last legs, and no one comes to see her."

I said, "Doris, I can fully understand why. She was a tyrant and made people's lives hell."

"That may be the case but do take her some flowers and grapes to cheer her up in her last few weeks."

I agreed to visit the nursing home where Miss Hack was delighted to see me. She didn't deserve it really. She had taught Mollie nicely enough as a teacher but when she became a headmistress she became a tyrant for some reason. (I heard that her sister had also become a headmistress but was quite a different kettle of fish.)

I started at Thurleston in 1958. The Head was a very good chap called Colin Bower. They had not yet received geography books in the school so I had to ask for some money. There were no wall maps either, so it was all a bit difficult at first.

On the way upstairs to the geography department there was a big blank wall on the staircase. I asked the Head if we could paint a map on there. We did North America with the USA and Canada and gradually, over time, we got pupils to draw the mountain ranges and cities on it.

At Thurleston I was also the careers officer and that kept me busy on the phone trying to find jobs for our leavers.

I was still Schoolboy Football Secretary and I organised a match called England vs the Rest in the early 1960s. The best Under 17 boys in the country were put forward to play against the second best, but of course there was not much in it. Some of them became England players and one of the boys even made the winning World Cup game. Martin Peters or maybe Alan Ball, but I can't remember. I wish I still had the programme from the match!

We played at Portman Road, the Ipswich Town FC ground. Johnny Cobbold and Alf Ramsey were in charge of that side of things. I spoke to them a couple of times whilst we were organising matters. Alf was a rather shy man and not terribly sociable. I once went to tell him that the Ipswich School Sports Association were going to buy a set of football socks for his team. He said, "Oh no, we will buy our own socks, thank you." Stan Frost, our chairman, was quite a bit put out by that.

The match caused a lot of trouble for me in contacting people from all over the country. A chap from Northumberland said, "Charles sends his best wishes!" He turned out to be one of my brother's friends. Small world!

All the teachers wanted seats in the director's box but there was not enough room. I didn't get to see much of the match at all as I was so busy running around after people. I had to sort out all sorts of accommodation requests for the visits as well. "We want a nice hotel near the sea side, and my wife is not keen on so and so."

"Bloody hell," I felt like saying, "I am a teacher, not a travel agent!"

With all that, and the work following up careers interviews and so on, I was told off by the Headmaster for running up a huge bill on the telephone! He also said I should spend more time teaching, but I explained I had to follow up these things to do them properly.

I stayed there five years and left in 1963. Colin was not pleased that I left, but our pupils left school with just a certificate from the Headmaster and I wanted to try somewhere where they did exam work towards proper qualifications.

Copleston on the other side of Ipswich was a secondary modern school that was doing exam work. I spent three years there under Ken Armstrong but also began some evening class teaching at Ipswich Civic College.

Eventually my Head of Department at the Civic College, Mrs Harding, asked if she could offer me a job, and I said I would take it if there was sufficient salary improvement.

When I resigned from Copleston, saying I was going to the Civic College, Ken said, "Really? Steve Burnell, my geography teacher before you, did the same!" And yes, he was still there.

Mrs H introduced me to the principal, Mr. Williamson, and I was surprised to find I knew him from my school days. I had not been friendly with him as he and his brother were a bit aloof from us common boys, being the sons of the Chief Constable at Jarrow. Williamson had been studying engineering at school but then clearly went into teaching. He recognised me too, as he said, "I was talking to your Headmaster at Felling, Mr. Youngson, the other day. He's a very old man now." I replied, "I thought he was an old man when I left that school in 1940!"

Williamson only offered me a Grade A Lectureship so I soon complained to Mrs Harding that I had come here to do more advanced work but was still only on the same pay. She went to see the Principal and they put me onto a Grade B salary which meant another few hundred a year. With that extra income we were able to purchase our first car which was an old black Ford Popular with a one litre engine and three gears.

I was teaching Geography at O-level and helping with the A-level. Some of my students were police and fire service cadets. They would be sent in by their superiors to get qualifications so that they could apply for promotion, but once they got the O-levels many of them would leave the service and go to another job! The Fire Service and Police were virtually wasting their money, I felt.

The other things I did were teaching English to foreigners and post office workers, teaching maths to nurses, and Liberal Studies where I got all sorts of people from all walks of life - gas fitters, secretarial workers, nurses and so on. The idea was to encourage them to talk about any subject they were comfortable with, let them loosen up and gain confidence, and get them used to talking in public.

I had to start them off on a topic to warm them up and of course some groups were better than others. Myself, I was always extrovert and happy to talk. Mind you, the first time I entered the big lecture theatre that held 240 people it was full of A-level students. I looked at them and felt I was only about their age. They were all yacking away, but when I put my hand up to shut them up that worked, and I got on fine thereafter.

There were some lady lecturers who did Liberal Studies and they taught a group of gas fitters on a Friday afternoon. These men often went out at lunch time for drinks and got silly beforehand, and they would take the micky out of the girls. They were a rough old crowd. I was assigned to them for a while and wouldn't take any of their

205

nonsense. I told them, "If you want to have a drink before you come in, that's up to you, but you have to come back to learn and if you muck about with me you'll be out on your ear, quick as a flash." That did the trick.

The college was newly built in 1962 and opened by the Queen. There was a fire there one day. I was up on seventh floor with my geography class when the fire alarm went off. I said, "Don't take any notice, it is just a drill." But it wasn't. It kept going. We knew we shouldn't use the lift so we all trotted downstairs to the ground floor. When we got down we found the fire was actually in the radioactive room, right next to where the lift and stairs came down together. The worst place for a fire, in all respects! The firemen were already there by the time we got down, as the fire station was only 200 yards away. They quickly martialled us out of the way and dealt with the fire.

With my interest and knowledge of weather I was asked to put together short courses of half a day a week for ten weeks. I put together three courses suited for beginners, intermediate and advanced. That was great fun, sharing my passion for the subject. I got all sorts of folk enrolled on this: insurance men, glider pilots, hot air balloonists, teachers, farmers and just ordinary folks who were interested. I had plenty of overhead projector slides, showing lapse rates, the rate of cooling as air rises, bubbles of rain forming, going up and up and condensing until they form into a cumulous cloud and maybe result in a thunderstorm.

The very first class I took was 34 strong. The deputy head came along and remarked that it was a big class. I said "Yes, they are all interested in weather, and it's a good job I am too!"

One farmer said to me one day, "What you are talking about is a lot of nonsense. The clouds come down the river Stour, and then they go up the Orwell."

I said, "Clouds don't just turn corners like that, they can't."

He said, "No, they most definitely do, I have watched them!"

He was not the sort of person it was worth arguing with!

Mrs Harding complimented me several times on the interest and attendance my courses generated. She was 105 years old when I wrote to her last year and I received a lovely reply.

Chapter 28
Stowmarket School & Field Trips

P rior to Mr. Williamson's tenure the Civic College principal had been Frank Metcalfe who left for a job in engineering education in London. He returned to the college to deliver a high-powered lecture to an audience of academics and local engineering businesses. He asked if anyone with a car was going near Ipswich Station, so he could catch his train, and I gladly volunteered to give him a lift.

It turned out we had some things in common and we had a good old chat. He was from the North-East, like me, and he had been a bomber pilot during the war. He had crash landed in the North Sea and got picked up, but then the ship he was in was crippled by a mine and they limped into Harwich. I gave him a quick rundown on my time with jet fighters, in return. I found out later that he had gone on to have a very distinguished war in Bomber Command. I felt very honoured to have chatted to him and that he had shown an interest in what I had been up to.

I was at the Ipswich Civic College for eight years between 1966 to 1974. By then Mrs Harding had retired and the new Head of Department, Tony somebody, didn't think much of me as I was the only member of staff who didn't have a degree, although just as capable. He suggested to me I would be better off teaching in a senior school. How about that for a gentle hint? As it happened, in the July Mr. Williamson came to tell us that the Geography department would be shutting down next year. We had to either find a new job or be made redundant.

I didn't care a jot what this Tony thought but I had already decided I wanted to get a degree. That took me about ten years, working hard in my spare time and attending many summer schools, until I graduated in Kelsey Kerridge Hall in Cambridge in the 1980s. I could function on a few hours' sleep and was happy to burn the candle at both ends of the day. I was also known at school for being able to fall asleep whilst standing!

After that warning from Mr. Williamson I spotted a top pay grade job as Head of Liberal Studies at Stowmarket Grammar School. I got the job and stayed there for 14 years, although sadly not at that pay rate as the Head cut all the grade 4 teachers down to grade 3 after I had been there a year (due to government cuts, perhaps).

Receiving my degree with Lois, who earned a couple of her own

Once our kids were in school Mollie wanted to have a proper career outside the home, too, and she began by accompanying morning assemblies on the piano and giving music lessons at the Castle Hill Primary School, working for Headmaster Frank Shiner. Her next step was to take five O-levels at the Civic College during the years I worked there. Mollie passed those easily and enrolled at St Osyth's Teacher Training College in Clacton to train as a primary school teacher specialising in music.

Mollie drove or shared a lift the 37 miles down to Clacton whilst I went 30 miles in the other direction to Stowmarket. When she had the use of our car I shared a lift with another teacher. It cost us a lot in petrol, being two gallons a day without fail. It was at that time Lois started cooking at home and doing the housework for her mum. Mollie didn't like cooking at all and readily admitted that Lois did a better job!

I enjoyed being at Stowmarket and don't wish to bore on about teaching, but here is just one tale from the teaching side.

The word had got around school of course that I had been a jet pilot and I was often asked, "Tell us about your time in the Air Force." Apparently more interesting than their studies!

In the liberal studies class I would regularly get an expert in to give a talk on a topic such as taxation or family planning, for instance. I always covered the Army, Royal Navy and RAF at some stage each year. I would get in a representative from each of the other services to give a talk and answer questions, but for the Air Force talk I felt qualified to do that one myself.

During my talk I revealed that Biggles and Rockfist Rogan had been my inspirations as a boy, and that my nickname had been Rockfist. After my talk one year, sometime in the 1970s, one of the boys called Andy Cubin came up and said something like, "Sir, I think I want to fly jet fighters. What's it really like?"

"It is great fun, if you don't kill yourself," I replied. "A lot of people do happen to kill themselves, but if you are careful, you won't."

I never thought more about it until, much later in 1994, I was at the North Weald Air Show. I was wandering about the static displays, enjoying the spectacle, when I heard a shout:

"Rockfist!"

That woke me up with a jolt... that's me! A young man came over wearing a black overall with a Leslie Charteris' "The Saint" image on it in gold.

(16 Squadron had been known as the Saints as they first formed in Saint Omer, France in 1915. We used the nickname "The Saints" and I had that inked on my kit bag. I think it was when Roger  Moore was "The Saint" on TV in the 1960s that the Saint's stick man with halo was adopted by the Squadron as we certainly didn't use it in 1950.)

I said to him, "I know you. Andy Cubin, isn't it? What on earth are you doing?"

He replied, "I'm the display pilot on the Jaguar in 16 Squadron".

I said, "That's my squadron!"

He said, "Yes, I know."

I was flabbergasted and so pleased I had helped in some way to inspire him. He went on to become a pilot in the Red Arrows, too. I saw him do a very polished display with them in poor weather with low cloud.

As I have said, Ronnie "Jock" Queen was a great pal. When we were at Gütersloh I saw him every day until I was posted off to RAF Celle and I never saw him again.

One year at Stowmarket Grammar School, the Army visitor I had invited was a Major Cork, and he happened to show a film about Army activities in Germany which showed Vampires rocketing and cannon firing at the Sennelager ranges, near Paderborn. I said that is just what I used to do and that my best pilot friend, Ronnie Queen, had been killed in 1951. To my great surprise, he said. "Queen? I was there at that time! I saw him lead a four of Vampires down into a dummy attack on some tanks in the trees. He left it too late to pull out and hit the ground and just exploded." So then, a quarter of a century later, I knew exactly what had happened to poor old Jock.

The famous football manager Bobby Robson was very good about giving talks to schools if he was asked. I arranged for him to come to Stowmarket one day, but as he didn't know where the school was he asked me to meet him in the centre of Stowmarket. He picked me up from the market place in his very new, powder-blue Jaguar which was a sumptuous ride. He was from the North East like me, of course, so we compared notes in the car.

He talked solidly from 1:30 pm until 4 pm with only a short playtime break. He was generous and most amusing and I do wish I could recall some of his tales. He was a very natural personality with the kids as well as with adults.

As it happened, Elsie Robson did teacher training at St Osyth where she got to know Mollie. After Elsie invited Mollie to visit for one evening, Mollie revealed to Lois that it was the first time she had seen a woman come home and pour a glass of white wine from the fridge! (But not the last.)

I got my finger in all sorts of pies. As a geography teacher I took the pupils on field trips and was very happy to arrange and lead trips abroad. A few of these stick in the mind.

The first was a trip to Guernsey from Tower Ramparts. I was No 2 to Bill Hummerstone and the Headmaster and his wife came with us. When Bill and I lined up the kids in the morning before we were due to troop off round the island and take in the sights, the Head would come with his wife in a pony and trap to say good morning. They would then carry on past us and we never saw any more of them that day. They just had a jolly nice holiday out of it! Bill and I were doing all the work, but it was a good trip for everyone.

One day we went across the water to Sark and started to walk around the island when we came to a natural archway. As we walked through that there was a rapid scattering of bodies... it was a nudist colony! When they saw all the school children they all dashed for cover in between rocks which made a very funny sight. At Rocquaine Bay we turned over rocks and picked up beautiful ormer shells. In the middle of the island there was a little church that was decorated all over with these pretty shells.

When I was at Copleston School I decided to take a party of pupils to Ostend, flying out of Southend on one of the marvellous Golden Viscounts. The Vickers Viscount was a four turbo-prop airliner renowned for its comfort and everyone was talking about these gorgeous planes.

My colleague was ex-Army Major Bill Ramsey. He and I had got these children down to Southend by 7:30 am on a Saturday morning for an early flight to get a full day in, but we found it was foggy and they were not allowing any flights out. The fog just lay there. Around noon I went to the Airport Manager and said, "Look. I have brought these kids all the way from Ipswich, to fly to Ostend, is there any way we can get up?"

He said, "There are no Viscounts flying, but there is a DC-6 going over shortly, if you don't mind going in that." I said I didn't care, anything that flew, and so we all boarded the four-engine DC-6.

Off we took, out of that fog, into clear sunshine. A little cloud, but beautiful. The pilot said, "Would the teachers like to come up to the cockpit?" Bill said, "You go, Ralph, you're an ex-pilot", so up I went. The pilot said to the second dickie, "You hop out and get a drink." I sat in his seat and the pilot turned to look at me and exclaimed, "Bloody hell! Hello!" And this was the guy who had embedded the iron bar of my flag in his Meteor at Acklington ten years previously.

I said "How lovely to see you! I know what happened. You got kicked out didn't you."

"Yes," he said, "I was bloody silly."

211

I replied, "I thought it was a big mistake to let someone of your experience go. I'm glad we are flying with you today."

He said, "Well you're a pilot, so you're going to fly it."

I said, "Thanks but no thanks, I can't, I have never flown a four-engine job."

"Nothing to it," he said, "I will look after the throttles. You fly her, and you just keep those two needles crossed on the instrument landing system and keep her at 6,000 feet."

There was a good view from the cockpit and good visibility over the channel, so I happily flew it along with no problem. I suppose one of

Happy pilot!

the crew had been overheard saying what was happening and it got about, "The teacher is flying the aeroplane!" Towards the back was a Belgian woman with her children and this intelligence gave her the willies, and fair enough too, although I didn't know it at the time.

When we arrived at Ostend, my pilot friend said, "You can land it."

I said, "Now hang on a minute..."

But he insisted, "Nothing to it, look. Throttle back, gently gently, take her down, just like we did in our jets, now level out... hold it, hold it... and we're down." Great! So now I have landed a DC-6. My heart rate slowed as my head swelled!

Then we walked out to get the tram from the airport and the Belgian woman was waiting at the bus stop. Bill Ramsey said, "I think you should have a word with that lady, she overheard you were flying the plane and was most concerned."

I went over to her and said, "Excuse me Madam, I'm sorry if we have upset you, but I was a pilot, and a friend of the pilot of this aeroplane. We were in the RAF together, so he let me fly it for a bit."

"Ohhhhh!" she sighed, and I could see her shoulders relax, a smile came on to her face, and all was well.

212

We flew back on a Golden Viscount later in the day, as planned. So, the kids got their trip (it cost their parents a bit of money) and I got to fly something new. What a great experience all round!

On a school trip

I got involved in the Duke of Edinburgh Award scheme at Thurleston. Mr. Cooper the science teacher wanted to do it himself for some reason, and didn't want me involved, but he and I walked the kids from Ipswich to Felixstowe across the fields, stayed at a hostel, then walked back. Following good feedback from that, Mr. Bower put me in charge of school journeys. First, we went to Switzerland, which was good fun, and then I arranged a memorable trip to Norway.

Norway was a most beautiful place. One problem was the weather. I had told the kids to be sure to bring thick clothes as it would be cold in the hills. We arrived at the end of May in sweltering heat and we were all sweating away! We couldn't put our hand on the side of the ship, it was so hot. A Norwegian teacher showed us round Bergen. He took us up to the top of the mountain there where we could see the long stone fish tanks down on the quay side. The fish were alive and you could pick which you wanted and the vendor would fish it out and prepare it for you.

We went up into the mountains and that was hard work for some. The way to get them up to the top was a big bag of sweets! Most of the boys were no trouble and usually shot ahead and got up there long before us, but we had to coax the girls up with a sweetie every hundred feet or so, and I still ended up carrying seven of their bags on my shoulders. We got most of them up the top, but not quite all of them.

We stayed at various youth hostels, one of which had a nice stream next to it. The other teacher, Derek, and I got up very early and we caught a trout each and the chef at the hostel cooked them up for breakfast. Being so fresh they tasted beautiful.

One hostel in the mountains was remarkable. It was a square wall with one entrance, and inside that was another building, so you could walk round inside the two walls, which acted as the insulation against the cold winter: the biggest cavity wall I have ever seen! The lady in charge was not very sociable to us for some reason, but she helped us make goats' cheese sandwiches every morning to take into the hills. They were gorgeous.

Voss was near a very old historic village. We went to look and were surprised at how small the homes were, with the same two-walled arrangement on a smaller scale. They had very short beds, only the size of a table, as the inhabitants would apparently sleep sitting up! The cathedral at Voss had the most ornate woodwork I had ever seen.

I charged the children £31 each and at the end of the trip I was able to return 15s to each of them. Mind you, I am still waiting for the money from one boy. He raised £21 from the Head's fund and I paid the other £10 so he could go, and he was supposed to pay me back when he could! So, if you are reading this... ☺

At Stowmarket I was in charge of school journeys but they were not very ambitious ones. Most of them were within Britain for the Duke of Ed. scheme. I had a group of girls who achieved their Gold Awards, for which they went to Buckingham Palace to receive it from the Duke himself.

The Head's daughter Catherine was one of them, so he was there in the audience. She started going green just as the Duke was approaching and I feared she was going to faint. There was a lady attendant standing at the side for just that reason. She took the girl away for a moment and I was worried she was going to miss the occasion and her Dad would be mad at me, but just in time she came back wearing a much safer complexion!

I told all the girls to wear big hats as I had noticed previously that the Duke always seemed to talk to girls with big hats, and sure enough he came along and talked to my six girls.

The Duke said to me "Do I recognise you?" I said, "Yes, Your Highness, I met you twice previously." One was a previous Gold DofE event like this one, and once he visited Stowmarket for some event. I was manning a stall advertising the school or something and we exchanged a brief greeting. I was astounded that he should be able to recall my face with the thousands he sees all the time.

Late on in my career my friend Phil James, who was one of the Maths teachers and a great help with the Duke of Ed. hikes, said, "You didn't know you had a nickname, did you?"

I said, "No? Unless it was Rockfist, I told them about that. What was it?"

"Rubberfoot!"

"Crikey. That takes me back! I was Rubberfoot back in my own early school days!"

I retired in 1987 after fourteen happy years at Stowmarket. My final salary was £12,000 pa. My pension after all those 36½ years was only £900 a month.

Hence I spent a couple of years teaching maths part time at Orwell High School. I am still waiting for the teacher's model answer books from the Deputy Head, from whom I took over! I suppose she took them home and lost them as I certainly never got them and had to work out all the answers by hand for myself.

I hope I made my teaching and trips fun for all my pupils and gave them some inspiration, as I did for young Andy Cubin.

I am still in contact with him and some others. Barry Aldous was very keen on 'planes and I took him along to several air shows. In return he kindly took me to Duxford last year, with his pal Philip Buckle, both ex-pupils from Stowmarket. Some things stick in the head: Barry's father had been a banana specialist at a warehouse in Ipswich!

Mollie retired from her own teaching career at Maidstone Primary School in Felixstowe shortly after me in 1988.

Chapter 29
A broken neck in retirement

We were both retired and, as always, we didn't want to sit around doing nothing and found some new hobbies and interests. We moved out to a bungalow in Felixstowe on the south Suffolk coast.

When I came out of the Air Force I went along to the Suffolk Aero Flying Club at Ipswich Airport. I joined as a member and told them I was already a qualified pilot. The chap said, "It doesn't matter, you still have to do our course to satisfy us." Unbelievably, they made me do a full 40 hours training!

A chap called Miller took me up first on a stormy day and we went right up into a cold front; he was really testing me out! But my IF was still good and it was no problem for me at all. I completed their course with various instructors until from their point of view I was "qualified"!

They had an aerobatic Cessna, Alpha Foxtrot, which was what I had my eye on. I used that whenever I could afford the £68 for half an hour. I headed straight out to Felixstowe and threw the kite about just off the beach: hammerheads, loops, rolls and stalls, so that Mollie could watch me from our garden.

I did that for years, sometimes taking a passenger to share the cost. One day I landed at Ipswich and the lady in charge said there was a complaint. She wouldn't say who the man was (but I later found out it was some Customs Officer) who had reported me for doing aerobatics over the town. I said that was rubbish, I was out over the sea but of course I might have been visible from places in the town. Nothing more came of it.

I took one chap down the coast to Woodbridge and along the River Deben at 400 feet which was wonderous. After the previous report, erroneous though it had been, I had to climb up again when I got anywhere near the officialdom of the towns!

A farmer called Andrew Williamson came to one of my weather courses in Ipswich and he brought along two of his friends, one a builder and the other a land drainage engineer, Bob Orford, who happened to be friendly with one of my brothers up North. The three of them bought a plane together. Andrew had his own airstrip and hangar at Home Farm, Coddenham. I became friends with them and used to fly from there myself. Andrew always insisted on calling me Squadron Leader! I remember a lovely but wet day when we went together to a farmer's fly-in at RAF Coningsby.

I carried on flying on a regular basis until I was 81 at which time I thought I'd better stop.

I volunteered to help the ATC at Woodbridge 432 Squadron, and others locally, teaching the cadets navigation. This led to the final time my commission was missed! There were civilian johnnies who knew nothing about the RAF and they were made officers willy-nilly, but as I had been a Sergeant Pilot they decided I should just be a civilian instructor with no officer rank!

A new hobby was fly fishing at Loompit Lake near the River Orwell. A friend of mine told me about it and I was on the waiting list for three years to join the club to fish with him. This friend died just before I got in, and I maybe even got his spot on the membership list, which was sadly ironic as it meant I never got to fish with him.

I caught six good trout one day. Mollie's piano accompanying skills allowed her to throw herself into a musical retirement and she played for a variety of groups, Amateur Dramatic, Dance and Choral. She was at Felixstowe Musical Theatre along Walton High Street that day, so I took my catch along to show her. Mollie wasn't at all interested in dealing with them so the choir master gladly took them. I didn't bother bringing them home after that!

The Probus club has given me a lot of enjoyment. We meet and have a chat once a month and have been on lots of visits. One friend I met was Ken Budgen who is now wheelchair-bound. He was in the Tanks for the Normandy landings. He told me they were in their tank going along the road lined with big hedges and were being shelled by the Germans. He needed a pee so when they happened to stop the platoon commander said he could hop out. As he did his pee at the roadside he heard a mortar shell which he turned to see landing in the top of the tank where the commander was standing and it blew them all to bits.

I was visiting Northumberland when brother Charles took me to a little village hall one night where he said we would play bowls. I scoffed, "We can't play bowls in the dark, Charlie!"

He laughed and said we would be playing indoors - it was carpet bowls. We went in to a packed hall where a big roster board listed names for the playing order on the two carpets. Out of kindness to me they allowed me to jump in to play one match of short mat bowls.

I thought that was marvellous fun and wanted to do this in Suffolk. I started the Carpet Bowls Club at the Old Felixstowe Community Association in 1988. I put a notice in the Association pamphlet that went through all the doors, asking people to come and join. We had a full house from the word go and had to limit the membership to 44.

I asked around and found the Adult Centre of the Education Department had a carpet and set of bowls which we could borrow. We brought them down from the centre twice every week to the OFCA Hall. We charged 40p a night and increased it to 50p until we had amassed enough money to buy our own carpet and a set of bowls from a supplier in Gateshead.

We played all the villages around and they all soon cottoned on to the fun which is carpet bowls, and this soon resulted in three local leagues.

I played for ten years until 1998 when we went on holiday to visit our daughter in the USA. It was our second visit; the first visit had been lovely so we said we would go again. Next door to Lois lived a Hungarian jazz pianist, about our age, and Lois arranged for us to go over there one evening so that Mollie could play piano with Eva. It was the most wonderful evening listening to them both whilst nursing a huge pot of American ice cream! At the end of the evening when it was time to leave, I walked out of the door we had come in through. To the right of the passageway were some steps down to the garage and I somehow stumbled and went tumbling down them head first. At the bottom I was semi-conscious as I can remember someone asking me if it hurt. It certainly did, but then I became unconscious.

Those stairs!

On the back of my neck was a lump like half an orange that was full of blood. They took me to the Lahey clinic where I was in their Intensive Care Unit for thirteen days, the first ten of them unconscious. I started coming round to find I had broken my neck (three-level anterior cervical spinal decompression), had a blood clot on the brain, broken ribs and pneumonia. They said if I had been American I would be dead. Other doctors, when I got back home, said I was a miracle and should not have survived that fall. I was 73 years old but I was fit as a fiddle and had just sailed through my latest pilot's medical.

In a coma in the ICU

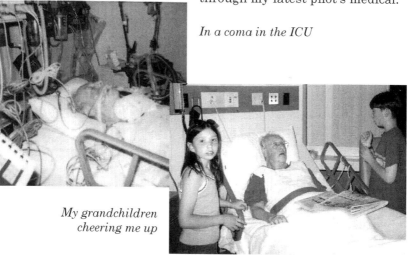

My grandchildren cheering me up

219

I returned home to the UK in a twin-engine Lear jet air ambulance. Another patient was in it already, which meant Mollie could not come in with me. Virgin Airlines were very good as they got a seat for Mollie that very day, so she could be there ready to meet me in London. The Air Ambulance landed to collect me and they asked for my passport. No! Mollie had it! But I had my pilot's licence and they said that would do as ID. They strapped me in with three bands so that I couldn't move. We went from Boston to Newfoundland, to Greenland, to Iceland and then Heathrow, and all that time of six or seven hours I was strapped down tight. Each time we stopped for fuel the pilots got out. I asked the nurse if we were stopping to get out to get a drink, and she said the pilots are, but not you! But I was only too grateful to get home safely. All in all, I was very lucky to be alive and to largely recover from such a fall. You can't see the holes in my bald head now as I had a cancer in that spot which was cut out to leave a scar there instead.

Before we went on the trip I popped into Thomas Cook Travel and said I was going to America for two weeks, not knowing it would turn out to be two weeks in hospital! I said I am 73 and I want travel insurance for myself and my wife. The lady said that would cost £120. "What!" I said, "that seems rather a lot." But I agreed to it and thank God I did! ICU was $3,000 per day, the brain operation with two holes drilled was $30,000, and with the ambulance home it was probably well over $100,000 all told.

Having broken my neck I could not play bowls for six months so I dropped out of the team and as it happens I never went back. I sometimes see one of my original members, Millie, who still plays in her late nineties.

Meanwhile Mollie continued her music until deafness and arthritis in her fingers persuaded her to give up, which was terribly hard for her to do.

I wanted to keep up with friends from the RAF and had many happy times in the Suffolk Air Crew Association reunions. I was Chairman for about twenty years in the days when we had 129 members. That has now dwindled to fewer than a dozen as my old friends are dying off. We organised trips and one time we had a go on Lakenheath's flight simulator, and all us old pilots were doing well enough but the chap in charge made very sure we all ended with a crash!

We had some marvellous evening meetings with food laid on by  Ivan Potter and his team. Terry Blake would play the "joanna" all evening non-stop with not one note of music in sight. Funnily enough he worked with Mollie when they were in their late teens and it had been Mollie who taught

A parade in Ipswich

him all about the theory of music, chords and keys. It was a shame they never played together to combine their talents.

I made some lovely friends as well as Ivan and Terry, such as Jim Betteridge who was our secretary for years, who had been involved in the Berlin Airlift just before I arrived in Germany. Doug Vince is one of the few surviving McIndoe's Guinea Pigs following a fire in his Sterling bomber. Gordon Garrett from Colchester was the only other jet fighter pilot in the group and I was fond of him. There are too many to mention

With my chum Jim Betteridge at Wattisham

all the others except perhaps Len Leeks and, of course, all the wives.

Other RAF contacts I try to keep up with are people I got to know over the years such as George Aird. I never flew with him but he was on the course ahead of me at Cottesmore and in Germany at the same time. We had several friends in common from Gütersloh such as David Garrett and my best man Bob Sowery, who he knew very well.

George was on 118 Squadron in Germany then moved to 111 Squadron (known as Treble One) and became one of the original Black Arrows, flying Hawker Hunters. Also in the team was Dave Garrett who sadly died in a formation accident at North Weald.

George became a weapons test pilot for de Havilland and others and became famous for bailing out at low altitude from his Lightning and himself smashing thought the roof of a commercial greenhouse... and surviving.

Last year I was diagnosed with various cancers and Molly was suffering Alzheimer's disease and her memory had gone. My kids took my car away when I was 90 and we moved from our beloved bungalow in Felixstowe, where we had been for 30 years, to a retirement home. We have no garden and greenhouse now, but we are well cared for by wonderful friendly staff and carers. One of the lead staff, Lorraine, happens to be one of Mollie's old pupils which is lovely.

Some Air Crew Association pals reliving old memories

Chapter 30
Goodbye, my love

S adly, Mollie never got to see this book as she died in her sleep on April 10th 2018, just as everything was being finalised. We had 67 years of marriage in which I always loved that girl and now I miss her terribly. I haven't got long to go myself, I am told, and so be it.

Mollie walking with Max and his dog

I am not a religious fellow, but maybe there is a heaven and when I go, I will be flying a Vampire in azure blue skies in formation with Ronnie Queen and other old chums under the watchful eyes of my dear Mollie.

Appendix 1: Family Tree

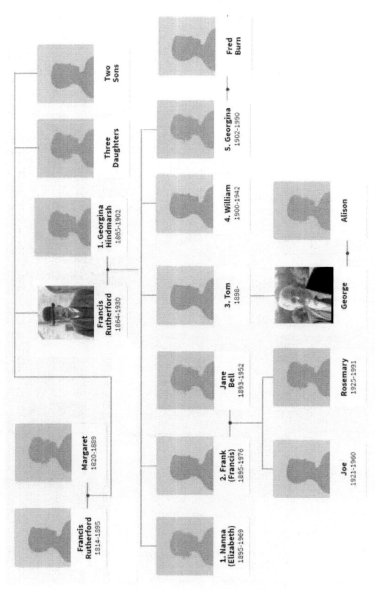

Tree 1 - Francis Rutherford's first marriage to Georgina Hindmarsh

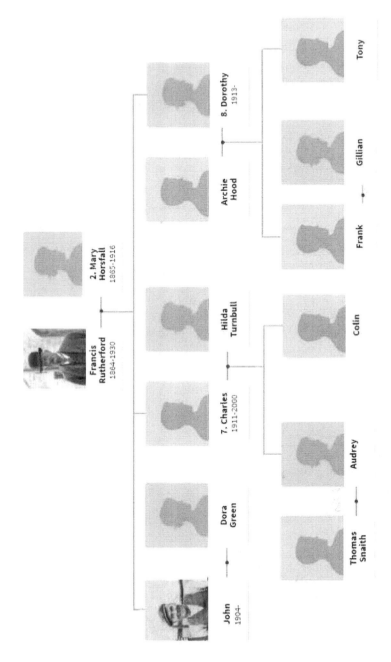

Tree 2 - Francis Rutherford's second marriage to Georgina Hindmarsh

Francis Rutherford
1864-1930

2. Mary Horsfall
1865-1916

John
1904-

Dora Green

7. Charles
1911-2000

Hilda Turnbull

8. Dorothy
1913-

Archie Hood

Thomas Snaith

Audrey

Colin

Frank

Gillian

Tony

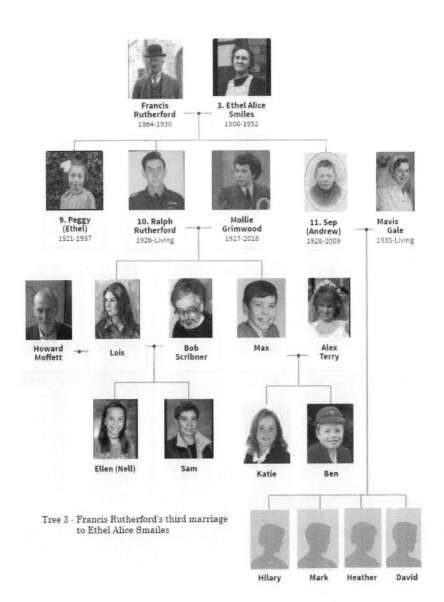

Francis
Rutherford
1864-1930

3. Ethel Alice
Smiles
1900-1952

9. Peggy
(Ethel)
1921-1937

10. Ralph
Rutherford
1926-Living

Mollie
Grimwood
1927-2018

11. Sep
(Andrew)
1928-2009

Mavis
Gale
1935-Living

Howard
Moffett

Lois

Bob
Scribner

Max

Alex
Terry

Ellen (Nell)

Sam

Katie

Ben

Hilary

Mark

Heather

David

Tree 3 - Francis Rutherford's third marriage
to Ethel Alice Smailes

226

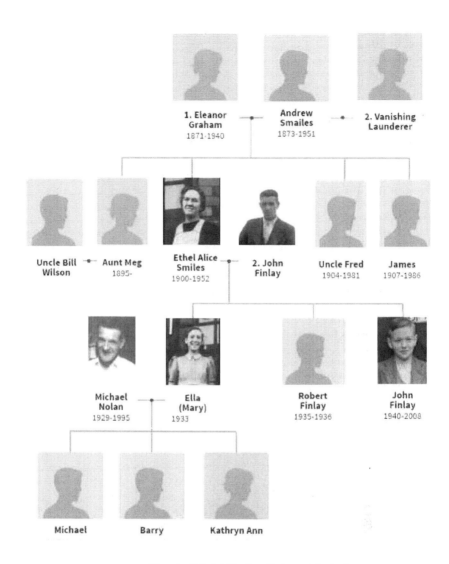

Tree 4 - Ethel Alice Smailes' second marriage
To John Finlay

227

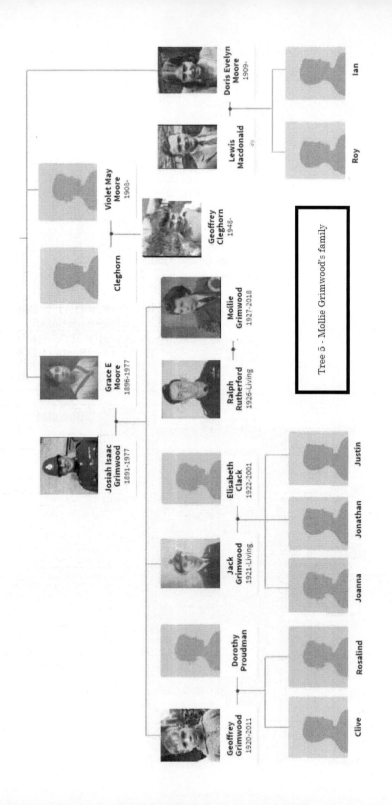

Tree 5 - Mollie Grimwood's family

Josiah Isaac Grimwood 1891-1977

Grace E Moore 1896-1977

Violet May Moore 1908-

Cleghorn

Doris Evelyn Moore 1909-

Lewis Macdonald

Geoffrey Cleghorn 1948-

Geoffrey Grimwood 1920-2011

Dorothy Proudman

Jack Grimwood 1921-Living

Elisabeth Clack 1922-2001

Ralph Rutherford 1926-Living

Mollie Grimwood 1927-2018

Roy

Ian

Clive

Rosalind

Joanna

Jonathan

Justin

Appendix 2: List of postings

When	Where	What
8 - 22 July 44	ACRC St John's Green, London	Induction at Air Crew Receiving Centre
July 44 - Jan 45	8 PACT Cannock, Staffs.	Pre air crew training
Jan 45 - Feb 45	Grand Hotel Torquay	Aptitude tests
Feb 45 - Mar 45	Pre ITW Bridgnorth, Staffs.	Initial Training Wing
Mar 45 - Nov 45	RAF Fiskerton, Lincs.	Bombing Up Lancasters
Nov 45 - Dec 45	ITW Bridgnorth	Initial Training Wing
Dec 45 - Mar 46	16 MU Stafford, Staffs.	Fill-in posting at Maintenance Unit
Mar 46 - May 46	ITW Bridgnorth	Initial training Wing
May 46 - Aug 46	11 AGS Andreas (IOM)	Air-gunner school. Got wing!
Sep 46 - Mar 47	RAF Jurby (IOM)	Air traffic Control
Mar 47 - Jul 47	ACHU South Cerney, Gloucs.	Air Crew Holding Unit (between postings)
Jul 47 - Oct 47	230 OCU Lindholme, Yorks.	Operational Conversion from Wellington to Lancs
Oct 47 - Nov 47	61 Sqdn Waddington, Lincs.	Not much flying
13 Nov 47	Jabs for Middle East	Sick!
Nov 47 - Dec 47	61 Sqdn Hemswell, Lincs	Can't recall
Dec 47	ACHU South Cerney	Holding
Jan 48 - Feb 48	3 EFTS Shellingford, Oxfords.	Elementary Flying Training school
Feb 48 - Mar 48	ACHU Sth Cerney	Holding, yet again
Mar 48 - Jul 48	2 ITS Wittering, Cambs.	Initial Training Squadron - 20 weeks ground course for pilots
Jul 48 - Aug 49	7 FTS Cottesmore, Rutland	Flying Training School - Got my Wings!
Aug 49 - Nov 49	240 OCU North Luffenham, Rutland	Ghost posting (Air Traffic Control)
Nov 49 - Dec 49	203 AFS Driffield, Yorks.	Advanced Flying School - Jets!
Jan 50 - Mar 50	226 OCU Stradishall, Suffolk	Vampire combat training
Mar 50	5 PDC Hednesford, Staffs.	Personnel Despatch Centre

WEST GERMANY		
17 - 20 Mar 50	Buckeburg Barracks (W Germany)	Arrival point in FRG
21 Mar - 5 Jul 50	16 Sqn Gutersloh (W Germany)	My new Fighter Squadron
5 Jul - 11 Aug 50	16 Sqn RAF Odiham (Hants, UK)	Exercise (Ex.) Hotdog and Ex. Kingpin
12 Aug - 2 Nov 50	16 Sqn Gutersloh	
2 Nov 50 - 3 May 51	16 Sqn Celle (W Germany)	Squadron relocated
3 - 31 May 51	APS Sylt (W Germany)	Armament Practise School
31 May - 24 Jun 51	16 Sqn Celle	
25 Jun - 2 Jul 51	16 Sqn Orleans (France)	Paris Air Show
2 - 11 Jul 51	16 Sqn Celle	
11 - 25 Jul 51	16 Sqn Wattisham (Suffolk, UK)	Ex. Flamingo & visit RAF Trimley Heath
25 Jul - 26 Sep 51	16 Sqn Celle	
26 Sep - 1 Oct 51	16 Sqn Twente (Holland)	Ex. Cirrus.
2 Oct - 7 Oct 51	16 Sqn Soesterberg (Holland)	Ex. Pinnacle - Staines raid on London
8 - 10 Oct 51	16 Sqn Celle	
10 - 17 Oct 51	16 Sqn Filton (Bristol, UK)	Ex. Surprise Packet, Salisbury Plain
18 Oct 51 - 7 Jan 52	16 Sqn Celle	
8 - 31 Jan 52	16 Sqn Sylt APS	
31 Jan - 16 Jun 52	16 Sqn Celle	
16 Jun - 11 Jul 52	16 Sqn Sylt	
11 - 12 Jul 52	16 Sqn Celle	
12 - 13 Jul 52	16 Sqn Wildenrath (W Germany)	Flypast for Brussels Air Show
13 - 30 Jul 52	16 Sqn Celle	
30 Jul - 13 Aug 52	16 Sqn Duxford (Cambs., UK)	Exercise Spearhead 2
13 Aug - 29 Sep 52	16 Sqn Celle	
REPATRIATION UK		
30 Sep - 9 Nov	UK leave	
9 Nov 52 - 2 Jun 53	RAF Acklington (Northumberland)	Target Towing Flight on Meteors
3 Jun 53 - 3 Jun 57	On Reserve	

Index

232

234

Author's acknowledgements

I hope you enjoy this story as much as I did in the making of it, despite the tragic and untimely loss of Mollie as the book was being completed.

Thanks to Ralph for entrusting his story to me and allowing me to poke around in is memory for so many enjoyable hours.

My thanks go to Ann Strange for assistance and support; Jemma Gooding for such a stunning cover; my sister Dorothy O'Grady for more fine maps; and to my kind proof readers.

I dedicate this work to my children, Lillian and James.

Hugh Gunter Frostick
May 2018

By the same author

"Tales of Peter Potter"
as told to **Hugh Frostick**

ISBN 9780995793804
Frostick Publishing

Available online from
www.frostick.co.uk

As recommended by
Air Marshall Sir Freddie Sowrey, KCB, CBE, AFC

Peter Louis Potter shares his eventful life from "clodhopper to cloud-topper and fire-stopper". His revealing and sometimes risqué tales range from Essex farming and village life, wartime service on Lancaster bombers, working in a mental asylum, and as a fireman in Colchester. Never short of an idea for a laugh or an adventure, and often bending the rules, Peter gives a wonderful feel for how he and his family lived and worked at Fobbing on the Essex marshes and the industrialised Thames, and farming near Colchester at Easthorpe, Fingringhoe and Mersea Island.

When war came, Peter ran away from home to volunteer for RAF Bomber Command, leading to many exciting episodes in Churchill's Secret Army and as a Lancaster rear gunner. Peter's skill as a raconteur has been well captured by Hugh Frostick in this highly entertaining account that gives a fascinating insight into life and war in the 20th Century.

"Mister Lucky"
by Ivan VL Potter
with Hugh Frostick

ISBN 9780995793811
Frostick Publishing

Available online from
www.frostick.co.uk

A bridge collapses before him... a child is thrown from carthorse into a pond... near-castration by bicycle... a Wellington bomber is written off...

Ivan Potter loves telling stories about his childhood and war service, demonstrating Secret Army equipment at Duxford and Parham Museums, and reliving railway escapades with his brother. When he began to commit his tales to paper, he realised just how many lucky escapes and coincidences had helped him to reach old age, and this is what gave him the title for this book.

Ivan is a Suffolk farming lad who got caught up in the Second World War. He did war work in an Ipswich factory, then joined the Belstead Home Guard where he was one of six young men who volunteered for a mobile squad with special training and a secret hideout in Bentley Woods. He volunteered for the RAF and completed training as a wireless operator on Lancaster bombers. Then followed a long career on the railways of East Anglia.

Hugh Frostick has crafted 93-year-old Ivan's many escapades into this biography, with many a laugh to be found along the way, making a most entertaining story of a long and happy life.

Your book next?

Frostick Publishing can produce your own story for you. We specialise in bringing your tales to life, with skilful editing to ensure the reader does not become bored with minute detail. We are also expert in drawing out tales from older subjects, and with clever questioning can fill the gaps to make the story flow. We dislike disjointed reading material ourselves, so we always strive to create easy reading.

Alternatively, we can help you to print and publish a book you have written yourself.

Services include:
- Introductory chat to give opinion on your story
- Interviewing and recording subject and associated persons
- Transcribing recordings (ours or yours)
- Scanning and enhancing photographs
- Limited historical and family research
- Producing maps and artwork
- Editing and proofreading
- Book layout (typesetting) and cover design
- Registering ISBN book number
- Providing proof copy and instructing printer
- Marketing and despatch by separate arrangement

Pricing:
Interviewing, writing and editing cost is £25 per hour. Artwork cost is £50 per hour. A travel rate will be negotiated per trip according to location. If you are far from Essex, we will consider travelling to stay with you or near you to capture the information, at your expense. The overall cost will be reduced if copyright stays with Publisher.

Example book estimates (from scratch):

Tales of Peter Potter (300 pages)	£5,000-£6,000
Mister Lucky by Ivan Potter (150 pages)	£2,500-£3,500
Birthday Biography with family history	from £ 750

Note: softback book printing costs are extra, around £3 per copy

More info about Frostick Publishing at www.frostick.co.uk